SACAJAWEA

The Story of Bird Woman and the Lewis and Clark Expedition

JOSEPH BRUCHAC

SCHOLASTIC
Signature

an imprint of

Scholastic Inc.

New York Toronto London Auckland Sydney
Mexico City New Delhi Hong Kong

*In memory of my mother, Marion Bowman Bruchac,
whose feet now walk the Road of Stars*

No part of this publication may be reproduced
in whole or in part, or stored in a retrieval system,
or transmitted in any form or by any means, electronic,
mechanical, photocopying, recording, or otherwise, without written
permission of the publisher. For information regarding permission,
write to Permissions Department, Harcourt, Inc., 6277 Sea Harbor Drive,
Orlando, FL 32887-6777.

ISBN 0-439-28068-0

Copyright © 2000 by Joseph Bruchac.
Cover illustration copyright © 2000 by Stephen T. Johnson.
All rights reserved. Published by Scholastic Inc.,
555 Broadway, New York, NY 10012,
by arrangement with Harcourt, Inc.
SCHOLASTIC and associated logos are
trademarks and/or registered trademarks of Scholastic Inc.

12 11 10 9 8 7   2 3 4 5 6/0

Printed in the U.S.A.   40

First Scholastic paperback printing, March 2001

Text set in Adobe Caslon
Original hardcover book design by Ivan Holmes

SACAJAWEA

The Story of Bird Woman and the Lewis and Clark Expedition

THE VOYAGE OF LEWIS AND CLARK

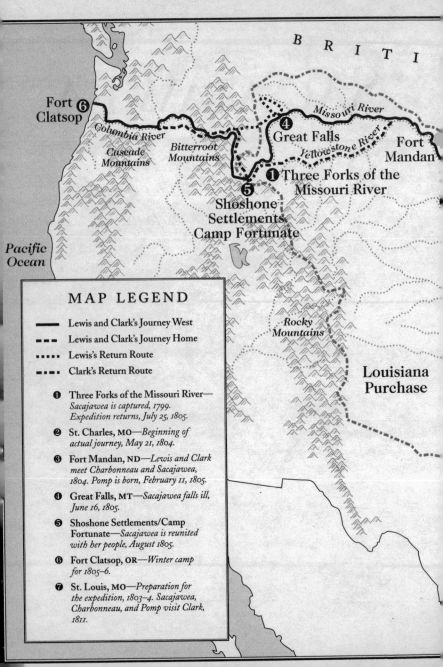

Fort Clatsop **6**

Columbia River

Cascade Mountains

Bitterroot Mountains

Missouri River

Yellowstone River

4 Great Falls

Fort Mandan

1 Three Forks of the Missouri River

5

Shoshone Settlements Camp Fortunate

Pacific Ocean

Rocky Mountains

B R I T I

Louisiana Purchase

MAP LEGEND

—————— Lewis and Clark's Journey West

– – – – Lewis and Clark's Journey Home

• • • • • • Lewis's Return Route

–•–•– Clark's Return Route

1 **Three Forks of the Missouri River**—*Sacajawea is captured, 1799. Expedition returns, July 25, 1805.*

2 **St. Charles, MO**—*Beginning of actual journey, May 21, 1804.*

3 **Fort Mandan, ND**—*Lewis and Clark meet Charbonneau and Sacajawea, 1804. Pomp is born, February 11, 1805.*

4 **Great Falls, MT**—*Sacajawea falls ill, June 16, 1805.*

5 **Shoshone Settlements/Camp Fortunate**—*Sacajawea is reunited with her people, August 1805.*

6 **Fort Clatsop, OR**—*Winter camp for 1805–6.*

7 **St. Louis, MO**—*Preparation for the expedition, 1803–4. Sacajawea, Charbonneau, and Pomp visit Clark, 1811.*

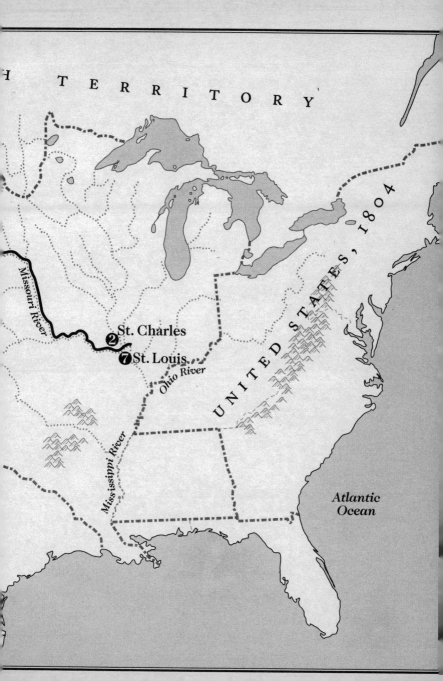

Prologue

JEAN BAPTISTE CHARBONNEAU

*M*y friends, as we gather around this fire, let me tell you a story. It is the story of how the worlds of the white men and the Indians came together. There is no one better to tell the story than I, Jean Baptiste, for I am of both worlds. I was there on that great journey. Now I am a man who has seen twenty-eight winters, but then I was a child.

It is a story of hard travels and many wonders, a story of bravery and kind deeds, of treachery and great danger, of strange men and even stranger places, of high mountains and rivers. It is a story of suffering and triumph.

I have been far since then. I have been to the schools of the white men, I have traveled to Europe, and I have made friends with kings and princes, guiding them to hunt the buffalo on the plains. I have ridden, too, by the side of war chiefs and shared the lodges of many Indian nations. Yet no kings or princes, no warriors or chiefs were ever better men than those who took me on that journey with them. Of all those who were part of that great adventure, there is one who was the bravest and best of them all. A great-hearted woman. Though she was little more than a child when it all began, she was the finest person I ever knew. That woman was my mother, Sacajawea.

But I cannot tell the whole of the story, for I was only a baby during those years. It is the custom of my mother's people, the Shoshones, that one can tell only what they have seen. When the Shoshones come to something they do not know, one who was there must tell the tale.

Those two voices who told that tale to me, my mother's and my uncle's, will now tell it to you. It is the shared telling of this story that is the beginning of my life. Now, brought back to life and breath are those voices, as I remember them in my heart. Here is my mother, Sacajawea. Here is my adopted uncle, Captain William Clark.

Listen. Here is our story.

1

SACAJAWEA

The Camp by the River

Long ago, there was a great flood. It covered all of the earth, except for the top of the tallest mountain. All of the people were drowned beneath the waters. The Great Mystery sat on top of that mountain and decided to make things all over again. He called to the birds, who had survived by flying up into the air, to help him.

"Dive down beneath the water and bring up some dirt."

So the birds began to try to do as the Great Mystery asked. The one who succeeded in bringing up some dirt was Chicka-dee. From that dirt, a new earth was made, and placed on the back of the big turtle. Then, from that dirt, new people were made.

ST. LOUIS, LOUISIANA TERRITORY, 1811

FIRSTBORN SON, how has your day been? I remember what it was like when I was a child of seven winters such as you. Everything around me was exciting, though our lives were much simpler in our mountains than here in this great city of St. Louis. I still find this place confusing. I am glad that we have your good uncle Captain Clark to watch over us while you and your father, Charbonneau, and I are here as guests in his great house.

But now that your busy day is over, perhaps you would like to hear a story? What story shall I tell? Ah, that story, the one I told you I would share with you only once we were here in the house of your red-haired uncle, so that he could help me tell it. It is a story too big for just one person to tell, this story of our long journey.

All right, then, I will begin in the place where I began, there near the three rivers, at the foot of the great mountains that divide the sky.

◆◆◆

We were poor people. That is how it was then, my son. We were not as poor as our cousins who lived farther downriver and toward the direction of the sunset. They were so poor that they had no horses at all. All of the other tribes called them Walkers. At least we had horses.

We were poor because we had no guns, as did the Atsina and Siksika. As did the other nations who lived close to the French and English and American traders. Those other nations, especially the Pahkees, the Blackfeet, they drove us off the plains and up into the mountains with their guns.

But poor as we were, we still had horses. We cared for our horses well. Our horses were like members of our families. With horses our young men could go back down the mountains and slip out onto the plains to hunt the buffalo. They always had to be on the lookout for enemies, but our horses were swift and our scouts were alert. On the plains you can see enemies coming from far away and escape. It is harder to see far away when you are in the mountains. So we discovered that day.

The day started off as a good day. Our village was camped at the place where the three rivers join. The sun shone on the water as it rippled and flowed.

I remember finding a little stick that was the shape of a canoe. I dropped it into the main river and watched as it floated away.

"River," I said, "where are you going in such a hurry? What would it be like to float along with you?"

I did not know how soon I would find out.

It was the Moon When the Berries Are Ripe. That is why my best friend and I were away from the camp, a short distance downstream from the others. There were berry bushes there. We were picking berries happily, and singing the picking song our children sometimes sing. You know that song.

This berry is large, I'll put it in my basket.
This berry is small, I'll put it in my mouth.

That day, as I remember, we had probably put more berries into our mouths than into our baskets. Our faces and fingers were as red as blood from the juice of fat ripe berries. Even though in our song we said the berries were small, I remember that they were very fat. All the berries were fat when I was young.

I had eleven winters. I had a husband already. I did not live with him. I was still in the lodge of my parents. But I had been promised to a man by my father. That man, my husband-to-be, had already made a gift of horses to my family. In less than a handful of winters, I would have gone to him. But then I would never have met your father. I would never have taken my first long journey. I would never have become the Woman Who Was Lost. You, my tall boy, would never have been here in the house of your good uncle.

How did we know there was trouble? My best friend, Wren, was the first to hear the cry.

"Enemies! Many enemies!"

Perhaps it was my older brother, Stays Here, who shouted the alarm. He was always the most alert of the young men, and it was said even then that he would surely become a chief. But by the time I saw him and my people again, even he could not remember who first saw the attack coming.

The first sound of guns came right after that shout. I stood there, unable to move. Wren tugged my hand. Then she tugged it harder.

"Boat Pusher," she shouted, "we must flee."

Then she was off, running away from the sounds of shouting and gunfire and the pounding of horses' hooves. I looked back toward our village. People were scattering in all directions like a flock of ducks before a diving hawk. They were too far away for me to join them.

I followed Wren as best I could. But her legs were longer than mine and I could not keep up with her. As fast as we ran, though, it was no use. The enemies had attacked from more than one direction. There, right in front of us, were more enemies on horseback. We were running right toward them.

That was when Wren received her new name. She turned and ran across the stream. With her long legs she leaped and bounded and was across almost as quickly as a skipping stone or a jumping fish. And as I would learn later, that became her name for the rest of her life, Jumping Fish.

I tried to follow. I remember the water splashing around my feet as I struggled toward the other side. I remember slipping on the stones and the sound of my own breath as I half ran and half swam through that cold water. If I could reach the other bank, which was steep and sandy, I might be able to scurry up it as my friend had just done. The horses' hooves would sink in the sandbank and slow them down.

But the sound of the closest rider's horse was right behind me, its breath chuffing. I could hear the thump of the rider's heels on the sides of his horse.

"Hey-yah!" the rider shouted, urging his horse on. Then he shouted something else in an enemy language that I could not speak. Whatever it was, his voice was too close.

I turned then. I knew I could not escape and I did not want to be caught from behind. What else could I do? I was a girl with no weapons. I stood there in the middle of the stream with my head raised.

The rider stopped just short of riding me down. I knew what he was probably thinking—*Good, now I will not have to hurt this one to catch her. She will be valuable as a captive. She will be one who can help my mothers and sisters with their work. Maybe I will even be able to sell her for a good price.*

I recognized by his clothing that he was a Minnetaree, and by the way his face and his horse were painted. Hidatsa, they call themselves. Then he smiled.

I spat into the water between us. I looked hard at him, wishing I could kill him with my eyes. But my eyes were neither a lance nor a war bow. So I became a captive. So my long journey began.

2

WILLIAM CLARK

The Corps of Discovery

We are to ascend the Missouri River with a boat as far as it is navigable and then to go by land, to the western ocean, if nothing prevents, &c.

This party consists of 25 picked Men of the armey & country and I am So happy as to be one of them pick'd Men....

We are to Start in ten days up the Missouri River.... We expect to be gone 18 months or two years. We are to Receive a great Reward for this expedition, when we Return.

—LETTER OF SERGEANT JOHN ORDWAY
TO HIS PARENTS, DATED APRIL 8, 1804

WHERE WAS I WHEN YOUR MOTHER was taken captive?

Pomp, my lad, you ask questions like a Virginia lawyer. Are you sure you are only seven years old? Yes, I know you are. As sure as I know you can already speak English and French, Hidatsa and Shoshone. But you still want an answer, eh? Far away from the Three Forks, that is the easy answer.

Yes, I am certain Captain Lewis and I would have come to her aid had we been there. When those Hidatsa raided the Shoshone village, that would have been 1799. July, if the berries were ripe.

But the first time we met your mother was five years later. November of 1804, it was. At Fort Mandan, on the north bank of the Missouri River, just across from the lower Mandan village led by Big White and Little Raven.

Why were we there? I will tell you the tale, a bit of it at least, today. Maybe more tomorrow. It is the tale of the best group of men and the finest captain I have ever known, God rest my dear friend's soul. It is the story of the Corps of Discovery, and your mother's story, too. Her life was as much changed by our journey as our lives were changed, for the better, by knowing her.

For me it began when a letter written on June 19, 1803, came.

Who was it from? Right, indeed, lad. It was from Meriwether Lewis. Captain Lewis, by then. When I first met him, in 1795, he was an ensign on the Ohio frontier and under my command. A fine marksman, as were all my men. His last commanding officer had not much liked Ensign Lewis. Even back then Meri was, well, excitable. Never one to be patient with a fool, even if that fool outranked him.

But there was no trouble between us. Nor would there ever be. I admired his courage and his pride, the spirit that I thought then could never be broken. He served only six months in my Chosen Rifle Company, but in that time the two of us became as close friends as any two can ever be. When we parted company he clasped my hand with just as much warmth as I did his.

"Billy," he said, "one day we two shall do great things together."

Now, if another man said that, you might have laughed. But not when it was said by Meriwether Lewis. So I just nodded back to him, not knowing how true those words of his would prove to be. Then, almost eight years later, that letter arrived. It asked me to take part with him in an adventure. These words I know by heart:

"My plan," Captain Lewis wrote, "is to descend the Ohio River in a keeled boat, thence up the mouth of the Mississippi to the mouth of the Missouri, and up that river...to its source, and if practicable pass over to the waters of the Columbia or Oregon River and by descending it reach the Western Ocean."

That plan, of course, came from Thomas Jefferson. Everyone knew that our new president longed to have the western part of the continent explored. Captain Lewis had been taken on as the personal secretary to Jefferson several years before, so that Meri could be trained to lead just such an undertaking. Jefferson also had an abiding curiosity about all things scientific and human. So we were to make maps, observe latitude and longitude, and collect specimens and information wherever we went. Making contact with the various Indian nations, both to know them and to civilize them, was to be one of our primary objectives, as was the arranging of peace treaties among Indian nations.

Think of that, the boldness of it. We would cross the continent and be the first Americans to do it. That in itself was enough to make me as eager as a starved trout is to bite on a baited hook.

The best of the letter was at the end. Though this would be an enterprise with its share of fatigue, dangers, and honors, if there was anything that might induce me to participate, he said, "There is no man on earth with whom I should feel equal pleasure in sharing them as with yourself."

Not only that, we would share the command. Two captains together, striking out across the continent. I lost no time in writing back to my dear old companion.

"My friend," I told him, "I join you with hand and heart."

3

SACAJAWEA

〈〉〈〉〈〉〈〉〈〉〈〉〈〉〈〉〈〉

Among the Minnetarees

Now that the snow has begun to fall in the mountains, Coyote will not be displeased if we talk about him. Yes, this is a story about Coyote.

Coyote was always changing things. He was not like Older Brother Wolf, who liked things to stay just as they were. No, even when things were good, Coyote had to change them. And he was so curious. Whenever he saw something new, Coyote had to go and see what it was.

That is how Coyote is.

IS THERE SPACE inside your head for more words?...Ah, that is true. A story is different. There is always a place for another story. Do you remember where I tied the knot in my story?...That is right, it was just when a Minnetaree had taken me captive.

Otter Woman had been taken captive, too. She and I spoke softly to each other to keep our spirits up as we traveled down the river trail. Our wrists were tied to ropes that were held in the hands of the cruel Minnetarees who had caught us.

That way, even though we were riding horses, we could not try to escape. Still, we made halfhearted jokes about how ugly our captors were.

"This one who has grabbed me is so ugly," I said, "that the only way he can get close to a woman is by tying her to a rope!"

"Hah," Otter Woman whispered. "You are lucky. *This* one is so ugly that even a grizzly bear would run from him in fright."

I almost smiled, despite the rawhide that was tight around my wrists. But I could not leave it at that. I could never let Otter Woman get the better of me, even when we were making jokes that might get us beaten by our captors.

"Mine is worse than that," I said. "If he should see his own reflection in the river, it would frighten him to death."

From behind me I heard an even deeper laugh than Otter Woman's. It was the Minnetaree who held her rope. His ears were better than I had expected, and it seemed he knew more of our language than we thought.

"Horned Weasel, it is true what this one says about you being hard to look at," he called up to my captor, speaking in our language. "I have seen how you always look away when you are close to the water."

"Be quiet," said Horned Weasel, the one whose hand held the rope about my wrist. He jerked the rope just hard enough to almost pull me off onto the ground, where the horses might have stepped on me.

❖

I imagined my brother and others in my tribe ambushing the Minnetarees and setting us free. I waited and waited, silently, but this did not happen. Deer do not attack a mountain lion, even though they outnumber it.

I knew that some of our people had been hurt and killed when the attack came on our camp. It would be hard enough for them to survive now that most of their horses had been taken, horses that Otter Woman and the other captives and I were now being forced to ride. We would be mourned. We would not be forgotten. Yet there would be no attempt at rescue or revenge.

Horned Weasel, the leader of the raiding party, took us along the river, across hills I had never seen before, and down into a camp far from my own land. And there I settled into the life of a captive.

I was shocked by the Minnetaree people. They were ill-mannered. Perhaps it was because they had been influenced by the white traders—those who have upside-down faces.

Did I ever share with you our tale of why the white people were sometimes spoken of in that way, my son? It is said that the first white man one of our Indian people saw had hair all over his chin and no hair at all on the top of his head.

"Ah," said the one who saw that man, "the Creator must have been confused when these people were made. They were given faces that are upside-down."

Those Minnetarees had learned many things from the upside-down-faced people. There was the food they ate. Not just good buffalo meat or deer meat or corn, but strange food. Some of that food was so sweet, sweeter than berries, that it made me long to be able to share it with the brother and the friends that I would probably never see again. Some of it tasted dry, caught in the throat, and hurt the tongue.

Then there was the way they dressed, with big cloth hats and shirts, mirrors and bright beads and other things bought from the traders. And the way they talked. Not just their own strange language, but mixing in new words I had never heard before, words I later learned were French and English. Most of them were words that men say to each other only when they want to insult someone or show how much they despise that person. All those things were so strange. It could not have been stranger to me if I had been taken captive by a band of bears dressed like people.

So we traveled down the river toward the trading towns of the Mandans and the Minnetarees. I was hoping for rescue, but as I traveled I kept my eyes open. I was learning about the world beyond our mountains. Little did I know then how far I would travel and how much of that new world I would see.

◈◈◈

What was it like to be a captive? I can tell you this, I was soon sorry that I had asked the river what it was like to travel. Remember, Firstborn Son, never ask a river for anything unless you are sure it is something that you truly desire. For when I was given what I asked for, it was not something that I wanted at all.

First of all, traveling as one held captive is not something to enjoy. It means having your hands and legs bound. Your wrists are chafed and begin to bleed. Your back and your neck become stiff, and even when you are allowed to dismount and rest, you cannot really rest. At any moment those who control you may decide it is time again to travel. And you have no choice. To be a captive means that even when those bonds are removed, you are still not truly free. For you still have your every movement watched. Those who hold you against your will know that, at first, your only waking thought is to escape. To return to your parents, to walk again in those familiar places where you picked berries or knelt by the fire and cooked with your mother. The places where you gathered camas roots, the places where you listened to the songs of the mountains. The places where you sat by the river and dreamed. Someday, Firstborn Son, I will take you to those places. I will show you the three rivers that come together. I may even take you farther and show you the river that the captains named for me, even though it already had a name.

Yes, our captains loved to name things that were already named. So it was that I became no longer Bird Woman but Janey. But that was later, and we must walk much further in my story before we reach that place.

After traveling many days, we reached the villages of the Mandans and Minnetarees. There I saw others who were captives. I heard many languages spoken and saw things I had not seen before. But I was given little time to just stand and watch. I was quickly put to work. Horned Weasel gave me to his aunt, Red Calf Woman, who lived in his lodge. She was not unkind to me, but it did not seem that she loved me. So, even though Red Calf Woman asked me to do only a little more work than my own mother had asked, that work seemed very hard. It was the sort of work I would have done gladly as a young girl among my own people. But for the Minnetarees, it was not work I could choose to do or not. It was work I was forced to do or I would be beaten. Tanning skins, carrying water, bringing firewood, such things became my daily routine. I worked tirelessly, from dawn to dusk.

Otter Woman was also given to Red Calf Woman. That was the only good thing about our captivity. We were together. Sometimes, as we worked together, we laughed and joked. But we were more careful with our joking now. Red Calf Woman did not mind. She herself was always making teasing remarks about the men. They could not respond to her quick tongue.

But if Horned Weasel or any of the others disapproved of what Otter Woman or I said, they could push us down or cuff us with an open hand.

At night Otter Woman and I slept near each other. Then we could whisper stories to each other in our own language. During the days we were forced to speak in their language. Later I would be glad that I could speak it so well. But then it stuck in my throat like a bone in a chewed piece of meat.

Some women who are captives seem to be quick to forget who they were. They marry into their new tribe, bear children, think of themselves as no longer Shoshone, but now Minnetaree or Mandan or Lakota. I vowed to myself that I would not be one of them. No matter how far I traveled, no matter who became my husband, I would never forget my own name. I would never forget the place where I was born and that my mother had planted a small fir tree over my birth cord. Like the roots of that tree, I was bound to that land. I would never forget the names of my people. Somehow, I whispered in the night, I would always return to them. And when I was alone by the river, I made my promise to its waters as well.

"River," I would say, "there will come a dawn when you carry me home."

How did I meet your father? Your father was not a young man even then. Even though he was self-important, it was said among all the tribes that knew him that Toussaint Charbonneau was a man of little courage. Whenever he met danger, he was not slow to run and go in the opposite direction.

"How else," he would say, "can a man expect to grow old, unless he runs away from whatever would kill him?" Do not worry, my son, your father will live to be an old, old man.

So it was that people gave him such names as the Bear of the Forest. That was how the Mandans called him. To the Minnetarees, he was Chief of the Smallest Village. The Arikaras called him Great Horse from Afar. Those were names not to honor him but to poke fun.

But he was also known to be clever. That is why he has always had success as a trader. He knows just what to ask for his goods, how to bargain, what to say at the right time. Perhaps your father's ways have been chosen by him to put our people at ease. A man who makes people laugh is always welcome.

And that is how it was that day. He saw Otter Woman and me and he immediately started making funny faces at us. Soon we both were laughing. He knew we were captives, but he did not ignore us or treat us badly. Though he spoke Hidatsa poorly, he was able to make himself understood through signs and the bit of French that the Minnetarees could speak. He said he would like to buy us. Horned Weasel offered to gamble for us, instead. He liked playing the game of hiding the stick inside the moccasin and was sure Charbonneau could not beat him.

Red Calf Woman did not like the idea. She did not want to chance losing the two strong young women who were now doing most of her work for her. When the soil had to be worked in Red Calf Woman's field with the hoes made of buffalo shoulder blades, it was Otter Woman and I who spent longer than any of the other girls in the field. When it came time to use the rakes made of sticks tied to a pole, we were the ones who could always be found scratching weedy soil about the short stalks of corn. But Horned Weasel reminded her that he was the one who had brought us to her.

"These two girls eat too much," Horned Weasel told Red Calf Woman. "If I lose them it will not hurt us."

So they began to play. Your father put a stack of trading goods up. If he lost, Horned Weasel would win that pile of cloth and gunpowder and musket balls. As Otter Woman and I watched, we could see how clever Charbonneau was. He talked and gestured all the while he played; he sang, tapped the ground, moved his feet back and forth as he moved the moccasins about, finally hiding the stick in one of them—or keeping it concealed in his hand. It was funny to watch his antics. Even Horned Weasel found it hard to keep from laughing, although each time he reached out his own stick to tap a moccasin or a closed hand, Charbonneau's stick was not there.

When it was over, Charbonneau had won us both. I was glad we were together, for I did not want to be parted from Otter Woman. We were so close. We had promised each other always to be sisters. We had promised that when we had children, each of us would treat the other's sons and daughters as her own. If we had been separated then, I am not sure that I could have continued to live.

Now we would both be wives to this funny old man with hair on his face like a bear of the forest.

"This will not be a bad thing," I whispered to Otter Woman. "If we are to live with a trader, we will not have to spend all of our days working in the fields in the growing season or chewing deerskin to make it soft in the winters. No one could ever make us work harder than Red Calf Woman did. And now, at least, our lives will be more interesting."

I did not realize, my son, just how true were those words of mine!

But that is enough for now. I will tell you more on another day.

4

WILLIAM CLARK

York

Sunday May 20th 1804.

The morning was fair, and the weather pleasent; at 10 OCk.
A.M. agreably to an appointment of the predeeding day, I
was joined by Capt. Stoddard, Lieuts. Milford & Worrell
together with Messrs. A Chouteau, C. Gratiot, and many
other rispectable inhabitants of st. Louis, who had engaged to
accompany me to the Vilage of St. Charles; accordingly at
12 OCk., after bidding an affectionate farewell to my Hostis,
that excellent woman the spouse of Mr. Peter Chouteau, and
some of my fair friends in St. Louis, we set forward to that
vilage in order to join my fellow companion and fellow
labourer Capt. William Clark, who had previously arrived
at that place with the party destined for the discovery of the
interior of the continent of North America....

JOURNAL OF MERIWETHER LEWIS
EVE OF DEPARTURE UP THE MISSOURI
ST. CHARLES, LOUISIANA TERRITORY

I HAVE KNOWN YORK longer than anyone. What is troubling York? Why does he seem so unhappy? Even I cannot always tell. We have been constant companions since long before he accompanied our Corps of Discovery as my personal servant—he ended up doing as much as any man among us. York's own father was my father's lifelong servant. I remember so clearly the days when both of us were smaller than you are, Pomp. We stole apples from the orchard together, shared them, and then shared the licking when we got caught, too. It is difficult to imagine a man who has been closer to me in many ways. Nor can I imagine what our great adventure would have been like without him along.

But you see, boy, York is a slave. Fine a man as he is, he will never have the same chance as a white man. It is not that he is any less strong or brave or even smart. When we had to decide our course of action that hard winter on the Pacific Coast, and we called for a vote among all present on our journey, York's vote counted as much as that of any other man—or woman, for your mother's vote was tallied right along with that of everyone else in our company.

And you should have seen him that first day as we traveled up the Mississippi and when we reached its big boiling waters. We calculated she was two hundred yards wider than the big Ohio before the two rivers joined up, and then more than a mile wide after the joining. York bent his back into the oars of the pirogue better than any other man. That is how he always was, taking on as much work as any man in our company and doing it with glad heart. I shall never forget the way he would laugh, even when we were in the worst of danger. His was a laugh big enough to shake the sky.

If he was to have gone off on his own, if I was to have freed him like some have done with slaves they have loved, why, it would have been no favor to York. Not at all. President Jefferson understood that. I never saw a man who cared for his slaves more than Tom Jefferson, but he knew, as any good Virginian knows, what freedom can do to a man or a woman who has not been raised to really understand it.

If I had been fool enough to give York his freedom, then it would have ended up hurting my old friend. He would have been confused, lost his way. He would not have known how to care for himself. He would have just fallen in with bad company. Or, worse yet, some of those damn slave catchers might have seen a strong, healthy man and figured they would get some quick money. They would have clapped him in irons, thrown away his free papers, and sold him downriver in New Orleans. I saved York from a freedom he could not handle. Be assured, boy, I love old York as much as you do. I will take care of our old friend and be sure he does not come to any harm.

How else did he aid us on our expedition? For one, York was a marvel to the Indians. Once we began to make contact with them, he became one of their main topics of conversation. Hardly a day went by without some Sioux or Mandan or Shoshone or Nez Percé or Clatsop coming up and rubbing York's skin to see if the color would come off. There was a game we would play whenever we came to a new village. We would pretend he was some sort of wild beast. York would run about roaring and grabbing at people as if he were mad. That would impress them something fierce. But eventually he would be taking part in games of skill with the men—and usually winning—or playing with their children, or being admired by their women. Yes, indeed.

Despite York's help, we knew right from the start that we would need another person to aid us. When we went up the Missouri River, we would enter lands where no white man had been before. There we would need a special sort of person. We needed someone who knew the land and the people, someone who could help us get horses when we left our boats behind.

Our time here in St. Louis was spent making ready. There were months of provisions to buy, trade goods to be chosen and bundled, guns and powder balls and charges to be readied, men to be hired. We were anxious to be on our way, to get as far upriver as we could before we had to stop and camp for the winter. Yet nothing could be forgotten, nothing we needed left behind. I packed and unpacked and repacked the boats at Wood's River, trying every possibility while our men grew more and more restless. Back in St. Louis, Captain Lewis negotiated for the last of our provisions. At last, near the end of May, we were ready, and we set out up the river.

◆◇◆

Bad as the Mississippi might have been, the Missouri was worse. Our journey was not an easy one. There were days when we would make no more than twenty miles, what with the currents and the bars and the sawyers, great trees that had washed down in the spring flood and then lodged with their roots in the riverbed, their limbs sawing back and forth in the water. There were always men keeping watch in front, ready to push off whatever was there in the boiling current and about to strike the keelboat; and men keeping watch on the banks, which were often undercut by the current. Great sections of the riverbank, as big as houses, would sometimes crumble in.

Yes, York was often one of those who kept watch. The fact that he was able to swim, something most of our brave crew never learned, was a great benefit to him when time came to leap into the river to work our little ark free again. Other times we would have men rowing in the pirogues with lines tied to the keelboat to tow it, while others were pulling from the shore to drag us along upstream.

Our keelboat was home for weeks at a time. I have only to close my eyes, still, to see it clearly. Fifty-five feet long, eight feet wide at midships, with a thirty-two-foot mast. And a fine sight it was to see our sail filled with wind, like the wings of a white crane. There were eleven benches across for the oarsmen, two to each bench. Many was the time we had to bend our backs into those oars. Many was the time our hands were raw and blistered as we fought the current or hastened to pull away from the banks before they crumbled down onto us.

There were a few things different about our boat, though. I made my own small modifications before we set out—while Captain Lewis was obtaining the supplies. I put in lockers running along the sides of the boat, devised so that when their lids were raised they formed a shield for the men on board. In the bow of the boat I mounted a fine bronze cannon, set on a swivel so it could turn in any direction. That cannon could fire a single lead ball weighing a pound, or sixteen musket balls, with a single shot. At my request, Captain Lewis obtained four blunderbusses. Heavy shotguns. I mounted them two in front and two behind, on swivels, like my beautiful cannon. They could fire lead shot, musket balls, or even scrap iron. And though we never had to fire them at a human being, having them there was a godsend. You should have seen the way we caught the attention of those bandits, the Teton Sioux, when we fired off all our guns for them. We were nothing less than a floating fort!

With all on board—the men, the tons of supplies, the weapons—that keelboat was no easy vessel to drag up the Missouri. And a long weary drag it was, indeed.

Was that the worst part, the hardest part of our journey?

Far from it, my boy. Nor was the worst part the danger from hostile savages, nor the biting cold that froze our fingers and toes, nor the starvation, nor the endless miles of walking when our clothes were no more than rags. Nor was it those times when we were so sick we could barely stand and the world seemed to swim about our heads as if we were underwater. Would you like to know what was truly the most difficult hardship for Captain Lewis and me? It was the waiting times. The times when every muscle in us ached to be on the move but we knew we were not yet ready, the times when we had to stay even longer. Those times were the ones that most drove us mad. We were young and eager, but for every one of those long, backbreaking days of our travel there were at least as many days of waiting and readying ourselves. And we had just finished such a biding time in our first winter camp. From the Moon of Freezing all the way through the Moon of First Flowers we were here near St. Louis. Our camp was just opposite the mouth of the Missouri where it enters the Mississippi. Camp Wood, we called it.

Captain Lewis had spent that endless winter haggling with the merchants of St. Louis for supplies—and dealing with their petty quarrels and complaints, for each one of them wanted to reap all the rewards of our sizable business. He did that and studied every map he could find of the Missouri upstream and talked with whoever he could find who'd actually been up the river, people such as McKay. That took all his time.

And what was it that I did? I was in charge of building the camp and keeping discipline among the men. And that was no small task, for a leader of soldiers is responsible for the doings and the health of every man beneath him. Some of the men acted so badly, stirring up trouble, that we feared we could not take them with us the whole way. Such men as Privates Reed and Newman were the worst. Others, like Private John Colter, straightened themselves out and made fine, reliable companions. At first Colter was so bored with the waiting he wanted to go back home. He was the sort of rough, strong young man who would do well in the wilderness. He only needed a teacher. Yes, Pomp, even grown men still need teachers.

So I asked the best of our men to take him under his wing—a man like you, part Indian and part white. He was the best frontiersman I have ever known, the son of a French father and a Shawnee mother. His name was George Drouillard. No, you shall never meet him. Like others of our company, my dear friend Drouillard no longer walks among the living. The Blackfeet took their vengeance on him one winter ago at the Three Forks.

◆◇◆

Now I will leave you to your reading. Mark my word, lad, learn to read and the world will open wide to you in every direction.

5

SACAJAWEA

Stories up the River

When the world was new, Wolf made it so that it was easy to travel the rivers. Wolf made it so the rivers flowed both ways. On one side of the river, the water flowed upstream. On the other side, it flowed downstream. To go one way or the other, you had only to paddle over to whichever side you wished and the river would carry you.

Then Coyote came along. "This is too easy for everyone," he said. "This is not interesting."

So Coyote made things more interesting. He made all the rivers flow in just one direction. He threw in rocks so that the rivers would be rough in some places, and made waterfalls so the rivers would be dangerous in others.

Why did he do that? Because he was Coyote.

Still, things come upstream: fish, water creatures, and people in boats.

And another thing that cannot be seen but is even stronger than fish and water creatures and the boats of people always comes up the river, too. What is that? It is stories.

I F YOU LOOK AT THE RIVER, Firstborn Son, you might think that everything in it always goes downstream. You see how the river's strength pushes down the limbs of trees and the small islands of grass that are torn from the banks. You see how its waters move so swiftly. But just as some things go downriver with the current, so do other things push up against it. You see how people take their boats upstream—how they paddle and push them or how they spread sails like the big white wings of birds, and then the wind helps them travel upstream. It is not easy for people to go upstream. They must work hard.

❖

That fourth summer since I had been taken captive, as the captains made their way up the Great Muddy River, the stories about them traveled ahead of them. Those stories even reached the place where we lived among the Mandans and the Minnetarees. What were those stories? Curious stories. Stories of a huge war boat that had guns on it so big that when they were fired it was like the crack of thunder. Stories of soldiers who came and told the nations along the river that they were no longer the children of the Spanish king. Now the Great White Father of the new nation to the east was their father. Now there must be a new way among their people, the white warrior chiefs said. Now it was wrong for the Indian nations to fight one another. Think of that, warriors telling other warriors not to fight. They actually ordered the people to stop fighting and said if they did not stop, they would punish them.

People laughed when they heard that. It was amusing. If the young men of one tribe could not go and raid another tribe, then how would they be able to earn names of honor? How could any young man of one tribe become a leader if he could not prove himself in battle? It was curious that a few handfuls of white men thought they could punish whole villages of Indians. These white men coming up the river were brave, but they were also foolish.

Other strange stories were told about them, too. It was said that their boats were filled with trade goods, with guns and powder and useful things. Everyone wanted to trade for these things, especially for the weapons. People understood trading. Even those tribes that fought with each other one season would meet together in peace to trade the next. For many winters other white men, British and Spanish and French, had gone up and down the rivers trading. But these strangers said they did not want to trade. They would not sell their guns or powder to anyone. They said they had brought all the other things to give away as gifts. But even though they gave gifts, the gifts they gave were very small. It was as if they were crazy.

When those stories came to us, we were not sure that those crazy white soldiers would reach the Mandans and Minnetarees. First they would have to pass by the Brule, the people the whites call the Tetons. If the white men would not trade with them, if they just gave the Brule a handful of little presents, the Brule would be insulted. Then those stories of the white men would stop coming up the river. They would float back down with the same current that would carry the burned remains of their war boat and the dead bodies of those brave but foolish white men, and their story would be at an end.

But the ways of stories are mysterious, Firstborn Son. And I will end this part of our story for now.

6

WILLIAM CLARK

Looking for Indians

31st of August, 1804—

After Dinner we gave Mr. Peter Dorion, a Commission to act with a flag and some Cloathes & Provisions & instructions to bring about a peace with the Seioux, Mahars, Panies, Poncaries, Ottoes & Missouries, and to employ any trader to take Some of the Chiefs of each or as many of those nations as he Could Perticularly the Seuouex. I took a Vocabulary of the Suoux Language, and the Number, War. &c. &c. This Nation is Divided into 20 Tribes, possessing Seperate interests. Collectively they are numerous say from 2 to 3000 men, their interests are so unconnected that Some bands are at war with Nations with which other bands are on the most friendly terms. This Great Nation who the French has given the Nickname of Suouex, Call themselves Dar co tar.

JOURNAL OF WILLIAM CLARK
CALUMET BLUFF, NEBRASKA

A S WE MADE OUR WAY up the Missouri, we began to
meet other boats, *cayeaux* coming down loaded with furs.
The fur trade, Pomp, can make a brave man rich or cost him
his life. For there are such Indians along the river as the Teton

Sioux, who have always tried to control that river trade. They may kill the man who seeks to slip past them to trap his own peltries. Or, like the Blackfeet in those northern mountains, they guard their own beaver trapping grounds with great jealousy. Many still took those risks and had been taking them for many years, going far up the Missouri.

On June 8 we met three men on a *cayeau* from the River of the Sioux, above the Mahar nation. Those men had been out hunting for twelve months and had about nine hundred dollars in pelts and furs. In but one year they had earned that great a sum. But think of this, too: In New York those furs would sell for ten times that much, and in China for ten times that. There are great fortunes to be made in the fur trade.

Valuable as those furs were, we were very pleased on June 12, when at Grand River we saw two more pirogues, one of them loaded with voyager's grease made from the tallow of the buffalo. Captain Lewis bought three hundred pounds of that grease, to our great and lasting relief. Immediately we began smearing that grease onto every part of our bodies exposed to the air. It gained us some small relief from the mosquitoes and gnats that swarmed about us so thickly that they almost blinded us and we breathed them in through mouth and nose. We would stand each night as close to the fires as we could, choking on the smoke, just to get away from those tiny creatures so hungry for our blood and flesh.

That same day we also met Pierre Dorion, a French trader with a Yankton Sioux wife. He was a fine old man and spoke his wife's language well. He had been friends with my brother, the "General," in Illinois during the great War of Independence. Realizing that an interpreter would be of great use to us, we asked him to accompany us, and he agreed.

Strong and healthy as we had begun, we were now suffering from boils and ulcers and dysentery. That came partly from the way our men would drink the surface water of the river, filled as it was with scum—even though we urged them to dip their cups deep, to the cleaner water below.

On July 21, more than two months into our great journey, we reached the mouth of the River Platte. We had come 640 miles and had not yet seen an Indian. The plains were filled with game, but not a single Indian, though we had seen fires and deserted campsites. One of our jobs was to carry the word to the many Indian nations that it was now our president, no longer the king of Spain, who was their Great Father. We had been given the orders to treat with the Indians fairly and to avoid conflict with them. We were to open the way for trade, inform them of our sovereignty, and establish peace among the many warring tribes. We did not know then, as we know now, that only the first of those three objectives would be quickly met.

Our flatboat was loaded with goods of all kinds to provide as gifts. We had beads, axes, mirrors, ivory combs, moccasin awls, tomahawks, brass kettles and brass buttons, calico cloth, scissors, vermilion face paint, tobacco, and whiskey, as well as medals and flags for the headmen. It was all divvied into lots for each of the tribes. We had prepared twenty-one bags for the tribes we had hoped to meet before finally reaching the Mandan villages, where we planned to spend the winter. Then there were an additional five great heavy bales of goods for the tribes between the Mandans and the Pacific. But we had met none thus far, disappointingly.

We did not know yet that it was the season when the tribes desert the river to hunt buffalo. But now we were entering the land of the Sioux and we would, before long, see many

Indians. And when we came to the Teton Sioux, we would see far more than we wished.

On we pushed, up the river. On August 1 of 1804 I celebrated my thirty-fourth birthday with a feast as fine as any king of Europe ever enjoyed. Here it is as I wrote it in my journal: "This being my birth day I ordered a Saddle of fat Vennison, an Elk fleece & a Bevertail to be cooked and a Desert of Cheries, Plumbs, Raspberries Currents and grapes of a Supr. quallity."

❖

Those plains were like the Garden of Eden, with so much game that we had to push the animals aside at times as we walked. One day there might be thousands of squirrels swimming across the stream and Captain Lewis's great joyous dog, Seaman, would dive in, killing and retrieving one after another for our pot. Another day there would be herds of buffalo or elk. Or we might fish, as on August 18 when Captain Lewis and twelve men took more than four hundred pounds of fish from a single Otoe pond while waiting for an Indian delegation to arrive. Hard it was to imagine that a time would come when we would freeze in the mountains, boil our shoelaces for soup, or be glad to have a dinner of scrawny dog. No, not Seaman, lad. He made it all the way to the great ocean and back as safe and sound as any of our company—all save one. All save one, God rest his loyal soul.

It was August 2 when we finally met our first Indians on the Missouri. A few Otoes and Missouri, accompanied by a Monsieur Fairfong, a French trader who lived with them, hailed us from the riverbank. Indians at last! It was hard to contain our excitement. We told them we were most glad to see them as we gave them carrot twists of tobacco, pork and meal and flour. In return they gave us watermelons. The next morning we met with them and their chiefs at Council Bluff.

Our men, led by Sergeants Ordway and Floyd, had been well drilled for such a meeting. To impress them we marched in close order in parade. Captain Lewis and I stood and watched in full dress uniform as our men wheeled, shouldered arms, fired a volley. York stood at my side, his head high in the air, proud to be part of such an impressive company. I must confess that the color of his skin seemed as much a wonder to some of the Indians as was our display of military might. I would later learn it was a custom among many of the Indian tribes to paint their whole bodies black with paint when going to battle. Thus they thought he must be one of our bravest warriors. It was a fine day for America.

Captain Lewis spoke then, translated by Monsieur Fairfong. The Otoes listened, impressed, I thought. However, what they spoke in reply was not great oratory.

"Very sensible," Sergeant Ordway said.

It seemed that they were not satisfied with the gifts we gave them. Each time one of their chiefs spoke to us he asked for more. One of them even came before us naked, begging for gifts to cover his bare body and whiskey to soothe his thirst. We gave him a small medal and a certificate.

I am sad to say, Pomp, that it was while among the Otoes that one of our men, Private Moses Reed, attempted to desert. He said he had left a knife behind and went back to retrieve it. When he did not return after three days, we sent Drouillard after him. Ten days later, on August 18, Captain Lewis's thirtieth birthday, Drouillard returned with Reed as a captive.

When the Otoes heard we planned to whip Reed they actually pleaded that we not do so. It was not their way to whip those who did wrong. As we would later hear among the

Arikaras, it was not the Indian custom to strike even their children. Their chief wept and pleaded with us not to do this thing. His belief was that if a man truly did great wrong to his people, then it was better to kill him or exile him than to take away his dignity by a public beating. But we convinced the Otoes of the rightness of our sentence, and it was carried out with the Indians watching. Then we celebrated Meri's birthday. Pierre Cruzatte brought out his fiddle and we danced until late in the night around the fire. Only Sergeant Floyd begged that he was tired and went to bed early that night.

The next morning, Sergeant Floyd's condition was worse. He was taken violently bad. Nothing would stay in his stomach. Captain Lewis, who served valiantly as the doctor for our expedition, had nothing among his medicines that could ease the pain.

"It is bilious colic," Meri said. Then he shook his head and clenched his fists in great frustration.

Every man was attentive to Floyd, York principally. York remained steadfastly by Sergeant Floyd's side throughout his last hours. There were tears in York's eyes at the suffering he could not allay.

On the morning of Monday, August 20, York and I were dull and heavy, having been up the greater part of the night with Sergeant Floyd, who was as bad as a man can be and yet live.

On that same day Charles Floyd died. We buried him on a hill that we named Sergeant Floyd's Bluff. There was a fine long view of the river there. We could see the way we had come together, and the longer way the rest of us still would go on without him. We placed a red cedar post over his grave. He was the first of our brave company to die, and we feared that he would be far from the last.

We had yet to come to the most perilous part of our journey. We had yet to meet the Sioux.

◆◇◆

Things had begun to go badly for us. Not only had we lost one of our best men, but a few days later Private George Shannon, the youngest of our party, did not return from hunting. No one believed that Shannon would run away, for he was always eager and happy to be among our company. But he was the worst hunter and the poorest woodsman. It was clear that he had become lost.

Colter was sent out to find him. He returned a day later with no success. Shannon could not be found. We could delay no longer. So we pressed on. On to the land of the Dakotas.

Our first encounter with the Sioux was with the Yanktons. On August 27 old Dorion told us we were now in the territory of his Yankton friends. A fire was set on the prairie as a signal, and soon a Yankton boy appeared on the other side of the river. He swam out to the white pirogue and spoke with Dorion, who knew him. We put in to shore, where other boys appeared, telling us a large camp of Yanktons was close by. Dorion and Sergeant Pryor set out for the camp to set up a meeting at Calumet Bluffs, a place farther up the river.

◆◇◆

It seemed a good omen, and when we reached that place two days later, we saw something else that filled us with hope. There on the banks of the river were tracks leading upstream. Drouillard identified them as those of Private Shannon. Thinking we had passed by him, he was following the river upstream, not knowing he was actually ahead of us.

I set up my writing desk, dipped my pen in ink, and sat

down to write out some remarks to be made to the Yanktons. At 4:00 P.M., Dorion and Pryor appeared on the opposite bank, at the head of a band of seventy Yanktons. The Indians were eager to welcome us. We sent presents over and told them that we would meet in the morning. All through that next day we talked. When the evening came a fire was made and their young men began to dance about it, telling of their brave deeds in war. They were bold-looking people, the men stout and well made, much decorated with paint and porcupine quills and feathers, all with buffalo coats of different colors.

Among them was a society of men like no other I had met before. They all had taken a vow that when they went into battle they would never give back, let the danger be what it may. No man of them would retreat from the enemy. There had been twenty-two of them at first. Just in that past year alone, eighteen of them had died in battle. They were stout-looking fellows and they stayed by themselves, fond of mirth and assuming a degree of superiority.

"Have you ever seen the like of them?" I said to Captain Lewis.

Meri gave me one of those bright, knowing smiles of his and nodded. "I can think of one group of men," he said. Then, taking his meaning, I laughed with him.

❖

The Yanktons showed great friendship to us, even though they, too, demanded far more than we could supply, especially guns and powder to protect them from their many enemies. We could agree to just one of their requests. We would leave their friend old Dorion with them. He would help them arrange peace with other tribes. Then, when spring came, he would guide a delegation of their chiefs to Washington. Thus it was that we set out toward the Teton Sioux with high hopes—and no one among us who could truly speak their language.

By early September we were in the land of short-grass prairie. On September 11 we rounded a bend and saw a familiar figure seated on the riverbank. It was Shannon, exhausted and nearly starved to death. He had given up on ever catching up to us and was waiting in the hopes that traders coming downriver would save him. We felt great joy, though I was amazed that a man had like to starve to death in the midst of such a land of plenty for want of bullets or something to kill his meat.

There were so many wonders to see in this land new to our eyes. For the first time we saw prairie dogs and that swift goat whose running is like the flight of birds, the pronghorn antelope. We finally managed to bring down one of those small, furtive wolves we had been seeing along the river, a coyote.

As always, Meri walked the banks more than he rode in the boats, carrying his notebooks with him everywhere, writing down all that he saw. While it was my job to pay special attention to the land itself, its geography, Captain Lewis had been trained in every other natural science. He was determined to carry a detailed description of all that he saw back to President Jefferson, who was like a father to him.

On September 23 the Teton Sioux found us. Three boys were the first. They swam across the river to greet us. The next morning John Colter came back from hunting to tell us that one of his horses had been stolen by Indians. It was what we should have expected. The Tetons, we would learn, are known as pirates of the river.

That afternoon, when a group of chiefs and warriors came

in to talk to us bearing a gift of buffalo meat, we discovered that we could not understand each other. Pierre Cruzatte, who had said he spoke their language, was wrong. He knew only a few simple words. More by signs and gestures than by speech, we tried to communicate with the Tetons. We marched for them, fired off our guns, gave them presents. They were not impressed. They were also not happy with what we gave them. Their three chiefs demanded more. We invited the chiefs onto the keelboat and gave them whiskey. Black Buffalo, the one we deemed their head chief, seemed willing to parley with us. But the one we called the Partisan was not. After a few sips of whiskey, he pretended to be drunk and was most disagreeable. At last we decided to put them in to shore.

They climbed into the red pirogue with me and soon we touched the shore. But then the Partisan refused to leave the boat. He pretended to stagger against me and pushed me. He demanded a canoe full of presents and threatened our lives. Three of his men grabbed hold of our rope and another wrapped his arms around the mast of the red pirogue. But I refused to accept such behavior. Thrusting the man back, I drew my sword.

"All hands to arms!" I shouted.

On the keelboat Captain Lewis readied the guns, aiming them at the great mass of warriors that had gathered on the shore, their arrows nocked and ready to let fly. We were much outnumbered, but we were prepared to sell our lives dearly. Save only one time, that one tragic time when Captain Lewis and I took separate paths, it was the closest we came to bloodshed on our whole journey. We would not go back.

But the Teton Sioux did. Black Buffalo sprang forward and pulled the rope from the hands of the three who were holding it. He motioned for the man who had hugged the mast to let go. The Partisan withdrew to the bank with his warriors.

I felt myself warm, and I spoke in positive tones. "We are not women but warriors," I shouted. "We have medicine on our boat that can kill twenty such nations as yours. We must and will go on!"

Black Buffalo and the other chiefs spoke among themselves on the bank. Then, as we started to leave, Black Buffalo and two of his warriors waded after us, asking to be taken aboard. They said that all they wished from us was respect. They begged us to come to their village. Finally things grew calmer and the danger was past. The next day we would visit their village, eat with them, watch them dance. But we would never trust them.

When we tried to leave, they again grabbed hold of our towline, begging us to give them tobacco—but wanting more than that. The two days we had spent with them were wasted. It was clear to us that these Teton brigands would still be the enemies of trade. And it is still that way to this day, my boy. But one day we will break their power.

7

SACAJAWEA

Little Mice

One day long ago, a woman was coming back home with a carrying basket filled with the roots and seeds she had taken from the granaries of the mice. When the woman heard someone crying in a small voice, she put down her carrying basket and knelt.

"Why are you crying, Little One?" she said to a tiny mouse on the ground.

"Big One, I am crying because my children will starve this winter," the little mouse said.

"Why will they starve, Little One?"

"Big Ones such as you take all the food we gather. So my people will all starve. None will be left to gather the roots and seeds." The little mouse put its face into its paws and began again to weep.

"What can I do to help you?" the woman said.

The little mouse looked up at the woman and stopped crying. "Big One," the little mouse said, "do not take all of our food. Leave us some. We always gather more than we need. We are happy to share. Also," the little mouse added, "you might leave us a gift to show that you appreciate our sharing."

"Ah," the woman said, "I understand."

Then she went back to the mouse's granary and put back enough so that the mouse and her children could survive. She also left a small present to show the little mouse that she was thankful. She told her people about this and they agreed to do the same.

So it is to this day.

WHEN DID I FIRST SEE the captains? I remember the first day we saw them. It was the Moon when the Leaves Fall from the Cottonwoods. Word had spread that their great boat filled with good things was still coming up the river. They had passed through the lands of the Dakotas. They had visited the earth lodges of the Arikaras, those who raid the Mandan villages from the south. The Arikaras had welcomed them and, it was said, made an alliance with them. Now the strange white warriors were again on the move. Their boats were coming up the river again. Perhaps they were going to join the Arikaras and make war on the Mandans and Minnetarees. Word about their travels had spread like a fire across the dry autumn grass of the prairie.

Then, that day, a group of boys came running into Mitutanka, the lower village of the Mandans. We were there that day, Otter Woman and I, along with your father, Charbonneau. He had brought us along to carry the things he was trading for.

"They are almost here," the boys shouted. "The boat with many guns is almost here."

All other things were forgotten. Everyone rushed to the river. Men and women, children and elders, even former captives such as myself and Otter Woman. Charbonneau, your father, called to us.

"Wait for me, *mes petites* wives," he shouted.

Otter Woman and I looked at each other. Then we laughed and ran harder, leaving him far behind. The strange white men and their boats were still a long way below the villages, but no one minded that journey. Our curiosity made the distance grow short.

"Hurry up," Otter Woman said to me as we ran. "Are you too fat now to run?"

It was true. You were with me, Firstborn Son. Do you remember how I always talked to you, while you were growing and waiting till the day when you would take your first breath? I did so then.

"Hah! The two of us can still outrun you," I said to Otter Woman. And then we did just that. I reached the place where the bluff looks out over the river while Otter Woman was still climbing the hill.

People were lined up all along the river. They were shouting and waving at the men on the boats. The big boat was not as huge as some had said. Some had made it sound as if it was as big as a whole village, so large its sides would scrape the riverbanks on both sides. But it was still very big.

While some of the men pushed with big poles and others paddled, still more men stood holding rifles in their arms. Their faces were serious.

Even from the place on the bluff where we stood, we thought we could see who the most important ones were. There were three men who stood out from all the others because of their height and the way they carried themselves. One of them was painted black, or so we thought then, to show

43

that he was their greatest warrior. The other two had hair that was a strange color, as red as paint. We could see by their hand gestures and the way they watched everything that they were the ones all the others listened to. Clearly, those two were the leaders.

An Indian man whose clothing showed that he was an Arikara chief stood with his arms folded right behind them, his head lifted up with pride. It was an honor for him to be brought up the river in this way. So he stood where everyone could see him.

Perhaps it was true that the Arikaras and the white men had joined together to make war on the Mandans and the Minnetarees. Or perhaps the other story we had heard, the one that was so hard to believe, was true. Perhaps the white warriors were bringing that man to make peace and stop the fighting between the nations.

Otter Woman and I raised our arms and called out to them, making those high ululating cries that our women make to call attention or give honor.

One of those two leaders did not look up. His face was serious and he looked worried. Yes, that one was Captain Lewis. But the other man seemed to find it harder to be serious. His head lifted up and he saw us and his face opened into a smile that seemed to have as much light in it as the rising sun.

Do you remember what I said to you then, Firstborn Son? I spoke it in a low voice so that Otter Woman could not hear. "That is the one," I said to you. "That laughing man with the sun in his hair is the one we will follow."

8

WILLIAM CLARK

Making Peace

31st of October Wednesday 1804

*the Chief of the Mandans sent a 2nd. Chief to invite us to his
Lodge to receive Som corn & here what he had to say I
walked down, and with great ceremoney was Seeted on a
roabe by the Side of the Chief, he drew a handsom Roabe
over me and after smokeing the pipe with Several old men
around, the Chief spoke*

*Said he believed what we had told him, and that peace
would be general, which not only gave him satisfaction but all
his people, they could now hunt without fear & there womin
could work in the field without looking everry moment for the
enemey, and put off their mockersons at night....*

JOURNAL OF WILLIAM CLARK
MANDAN VILLAGES, NORTH DAKOTA

No, POMP, IF JANEY, YOUR MOTHER, was there along
the riverbank waving at us, I did not see her. Or, if I did,
I did not know who she was then. You must remember how
great the confusion was. We had passed one deserted village
after another as we came up the river. Smallpox had struck the
Mandans and Arikaras well before our visit. Where once,
only twenty years before, there had been eighteen villages of

Mandans, now only two remained. The sickness was brought to them by the Spanish. Smallpox is a terrible sickness, Pomp. Whole villages die when it comes among them.

But we were prepared for smallpox. Look here, upon my arm. You see this small round scar? If you scrape your arm to make it bleed, then rub in some of the matter from cowpox, the smallpox will not harm you. President Jefferson had told us that we must prepare ourselves this way, to protect both ourselves and the Indians we would meet. We had even thought to bring some of the cowpox matter along with us to administer to the Indians. One of our great men, Attorney General Levi Lincoln, had suggested this. But Doctor Rush, the one who fitted up Meri so well with his thunder pills and all the other medicines, was not able to provide it to us. How does it work? Well, my boy, think of it as a good luck charm or a helper. What, Pomp? A *poha*. Is that how you say it, *poha*? Yes, it is a power. Yes, like the pouch your mother has placed around your neck to protect you.

◄►

But let me continue with my tale of how we came to the Mandans. Suddenly, after no Indians at all, they were everywhere, on both sides of the river. Men and women alike, they shouted at us from the riverbanks, watched us from the high bluffs. They waved for us to come in. But we were careful. We did not know yet what these Mandans intended.

Why were we uncertain? After our perilous encounter with the Sioux, we had come to the Arikaras. We found them a totally different people. They were not bullies and thieves. They were friendly to us, open to the cause of peace.

"No one," said Chief Kakawissassa, "would ever dare to put a hand upon the rope of your boat. No!"

The road to peace, said the Arikaras, was open among them. They were good people, they said. But the Mandans, they said, were not. Those Mandans that we hoped to spend our winter among, the Arikaras told us, were not trustworthy. They were dangerous people. But because we had asked and we were their friends, the Arikaras said they would try to make peace with them. So it was that one of the Arikara chiefs agreed to come with us on our boat. He would speak to the Mandans about peace with us and with his people. But, he told us, we must be wary. And so we were.

There were other things we had to worry about, too. Not only might the Indians be unfriendly, there were white traders there who could be our enemies. You see, my boy, there are different kinds of white men. We are Americans. Americans can be trusted. But those white men already on the upper Missouri were not Americans. They were Frenchmen and Canadians and Englishmen. We had just fought a war to gain our freedom from the Englishmen, and we may yet fight another war against the English. The English like nothing better than to stir up the Indians who would otherwise be our friends. Captain Lewis, in particular, spoke often about how we must not trust the English.

Remember, too, Pomp, what we were doing. We were coming to tell all the tribes that they must trade with the Americans who would follow us. They must no longer deal with the French or the English. Because of us those English and Canadians who worked for the Northwest Company would lose their trade. So we had to worry about what those other white men would do.

Soon the winter would be upon us and the waters would freeze. We could travel no farther. This was where we had planned to stay. But we needed to be safe while we lived there.

One of our first thoughts was to build a strong fort so that we would be secure through the winter.

On October 26 we camped in a cornfield just below the lower Mandan village. Our plan was to have a great parley with all of the chiefs of the villages. You know, Pomp, there were five villages then, just as now. Two of them are Mandan and the other three are Hidatsa, those people your mother calls the Minnetarees. The Mandan chiefs came to our camp and smoked with me. This was a good sign.

So the next morning, a Saturday, I hiked up to the lower village of Mitutanka. I climbed the fifty-foot terrace to the village. I surveyed the palisaded wall, the many lodges like beehives placed upon the ground, the hundreds of horses. As Indians go, the Mandans are weathy people. Their villages are the heart of trade for all of the plains. I was hopeful of success, but then a strange thing happened. They led me past a tall post standing in the open area in the center of their circle of lodges. I grew dizzy as I stepped down into the big lodge, which was dug almost as deep as a man's grave into the prairie soil. So I started things off badly. I did not accept the food they offered me. The sight of corn and beans made me feel ill. But only enemies refuse food that is offered to them.

"Do you not trust us?" Little Raven asked. "Do you think our food is poisoned?"

I was able to convince them I was indisposed and they forgave my bad manners. A free trader with the Northwest Company was also present. His name was Jessaume and he claimed to be a dear friend of my brother, the "General." It was a claim that I doubted. Jessaume was a cunning, insolent man whom my brother would not have liked. But he was married to a Mandan woman and spoke their language. An interpreter was sorely needed. Jessaume proved to be useful then and throughout the winter.

It was Jessaume who told us that another of the Frenchmen there had a wife who came from the Snake nation, far up the river. Those were the very people from whom we hoped to get horses. We were eager to make the acquaintance of that man, Charbonneau, and his wife. Such a woman who knew the land and the people would be of great use. Perhaps we could persuade her and her husband to accompany us. But first we had to meet with the chiefs of the village.

A meeting was set for the following day, but the wind blew down from the northwest so strongly that the chiefs could not cross the river to our side. The next day was no better. The sand came blowing in on us in clouds. But we tied a sail to make an awning to protect us from the wind. Then, though fewer than half the chiefs from the two tribes were there, we had our meeting.

It seemed to us that things went well. Captain Lewis made his speech. Jessaume interpreted for us. Those gathered there listened and agreed. They would no longer make war with the Arikaras. The pipe was smoked between the Arikara chief, the Mandans, and the Hidatsas. We gave them medals, and the bonds of peace seemed to be firm.

We did not know that Big Man, one of the chiefs of the Mandans, sought out the Arikara chief after the meeting.

"Hear me," Big Man said to him, "we do not trust you people. The two soldier chiefs have asked us to make peace. We have done so, but we remember how you and the Sioux always attacked us in the past. We know you will do it again. But remember this, when you make war on the Mandans we kill you like buffalo."

9

SACAJAWEA

The White Men's Fort

Long ago, the sun was hotter than it is today. Everything on earth was burned by the sun. One day Jackrabbit decided to do something.

"I will go and find the place where Sun lives," Jackrabbit said.

Jackrabbit had only three legs and could not move fast. So he made himself another leg out of a piece of wood. Then he was able to run faster than the wind. He took his bow and arrows and he ran toward the place where Sun lives. The closer he came, the hotter it got. It got so hot that it burned Jackrabbit's fur. To this day, Jackrabbit's fur is still blackened in places.

"I have to find shelter," Jackrabbit said. Then he looked around for something that was not burned by the sun and he saw the cactus. So he made himself a house out of cactus. To this day, Jackrabbit likes to live among the cactus.

In this cactus house it was shady and the sun no longer burned him. He waited there until it was night. Then, when night came, he traveled again toward the place where Sun lives. He hid with his bow and arrow and waited until

*dawn. When Sun started to come up, Jackrabbit shot an arrow
and killed Sun.*

*Then Jackrabbit took Sun apart. From different parts of
Sun he made the stars and the moon. From Sun's heart he
made the darkness. Then he brought Sun back to life.*

*"From now on," Jackrabbit said to Sun, "because you have
been changed, you will never be too hot again."*

And that is the way of things to this day.

EVERYTHING CHANGED after the white men came to
the Mandan villages. As the wife of a trader, I was no
longer seen as a captive. I was now freer to move about as I
wished than I had been when I had first been captured.

As you know, my son, among our people a person who is a
captive is treated much like everyone else in the village—
though more closely watched. It is not as it is among the white
men with their slaves, who are kept in chains. Though Otter
Woman was closer to my heart than any other woman, I had
many friends among the Mandan women. We shared stories
and gossip every day. Most of that gossip was about the Americans.

After all I had experienced, I was not at all afraid of these
white men. Everyone was curious about what those strange
white men, the Americans, would do next, including your father. They were all he could talk about. One day he would talk
about their boats and their fine guns. The next day he would
talk about all of their provisions and the plans they had made
to travel far upriver.

"How far?" I asked. "Will they reach the Three Forks?" My

heart was beating fast at the thought of those white men traveling to the lands of my people.

Charbonneau laughed. "There and beyond. They will go, they say, as far as the Great Salt Water." Then he looked thoughtful. "Before I die," he said, "that salt water I would like to see."

News traveled fast between the three Minnetaree and two Mandan villages along the Muddy River. After all, those villages are close to one another. One could walk from one village to the next in less time than it takes for the sun to move the width of two hands across the sky. So it was that word came to Meteharta, the Minnetaree village on the Knife River where we were then living, that the Americans were building something. Everyone was curious about that, especially your father.

Your father, Pomp, is always interested in seeing something new. Perhaps that is why he will never settle in any one place. Even though our friend the good captain has helped us get good land here, I know we will not stay.

So it was that Charbonneau decided to see for himself. His friend Jessaume, who was already staying with the Americans, had come to visit us.

"They are like big children," Jessaume said. "It is easy to deceive them." Then he smiled. "They deceive themselves. They think they can stop the savages from fighting with each other by giving them medals and flags."

"*Sacre!* Is this so?" said your father.

Jessaume laughed. "But their pay is good. Come to their fort, *mon ami.* They will hire you, it is certain." He looked over at me. I said nothing, but I was listening, as I always do. "Because of her," Jessaume said. "Their plan is to go up the Missouri to reach the ocean. But when they come to the river's end they will need horses. You know what people live there at the river's end."

Charbonneau looked over at me, a clever look on his face. He made the sign for my people, the movement of a hand like that of a snake crawling.

It is the movement our own people make to mean the weaving together of brush to make our lodges. But others who saw it thought it meant the snake. So it was that the other tribes and the white people called us Snake Indians. Remember, Firstborn Son, that *Snake* is not our name. We are the Numi, the human beings. We are the Akaitikka, the Eaters of Salmon.

"Yes," Jessaume said. "They need someone who can speak to the Snake Indians. They will need your Bird Woman."

My thoughts had already traveled far, carrying me upriver with the Americans, back to that homeland from which I had been stolen. *Yes*, I thought. *Yes!* But I kept my face calm and said nothing.

So your father went to visit the captains that very day. They had just chosen the site for their fort the day before that, and they were still cutting trees. So many trees.

I remember when I first saw the fort. It was a surprise. The captains and their men were not going to live in earth lodges like the Mandans, or even tipis made of buffalo skin. Instead, their houses were to be made of wood, nothing but wood. Your good uncle would explain it to me later. In his homeland of Virginia, they have too many trees. It is not like it was that winter along the Missouri River, where trees are not easy to find. It seemed that they were cutting down every tree in the world to make their fort!

Your father was welcomed when he came to Fort Mandan. Jessaume had spoken about him to the captains. He had told them that your father had a wife who was a Shoshone and could also speak Minnetaree.

"I myself," your father said to them, "I speak all languages equally well. For you I will translate them as you travel."

The captains listened to him with great seriousness—though I learned later that they found it hard not to laugh at his boasting. He did not really fool them, but they had learned how important it was to have someone who could translate for them. They knew how useful I would be to them if I was truly Shoshone, as he said. They hired him that same day...and told him to bring his family along.

Your second mother, Otter Woman, and I went to look at their fort soon after. They were making two rows of houses facing each other. Those houses were not round, like a real house, but had sharp edges. The roofs were not high, no taller than the height a man could reach with an outstretched arm. But the walls around were very tall. They looked to be four times my own height.

Seeing those walls, I wondered if what I had heard more than one Minnetaree saying about the Americans were true. They said that the white people did not really want peace. That was why they had so many guns of all sizes. That was why they would not sell guns or powder or shot to the Indians. Perhaps once the strong walls were finished, these white people intended to make war on the Minnetarees. It was rumored that any Hidatsa who came to the fort would be killed.

The Minnetarees were angry at the Americans because they would not sell any of their guns.

"The only ones who have any sense," a Minnetaree chief said, "are the worker of iron and the mender of guns."

"If we catch any of those white men out on the prairie," one young warrior said, "we will kill them like birds."

The captains would learn later that those rumors were being spread by the Mandans. The Mandans wanted to keep all the trade to themselves. They did not want the Minnetarees coming and getting the trade goods from the white men. So the Mandans told the Minnetarees that the white men did not like them.

The day we visited was not a happy day for your good uncle, though it started well when he met us. I remember how friendly he was. Jessaume was near him. He took Captain Clark's arm, pointed at us, and said something. A big smile came over your good uncle's face as he looked at me, right at me! Then he came over to us so quickly that he almost ran. He was such a tall man, Otter Woman and I had to lean our heads back to look up at him. He gave us presents, a mirror and some cloth. We were both excited, but we tried not to show any expression. I made the sign for thanks and nodded back to him. He just kept smiling, making gestures, saying things in his strange language. He really was like a big child, as open and friendly as one. I liked him.

But his face changed quickly when a Mandan messenger came up to him and Jessaume translated for him what the man had to say. It was not good news. The Arikaras had done as the two captains told them. They had sent messengers to the Sioux, telling them that they wished to follow the Americans' plan to end warfare among all the river tribes. They had asked the Sioux to do the same. The Sioux had whipped the messengers, called them dogs and little girls. The Sioux were angry because the Arikaras had made peace with the Mandans. Then the Sioux had taken away their horses and forced the messengers to walk back home.

Only the white men were surprised by this. We had all known peace was not an idea the Sioux would like. Before long, we thought, the Arikara and the Sioux would again begin raiding the Mandan villages, peace agreement or no peace agreement. So when the captains invited your father to move into Fort Mandan and bring his family, he was happy to accept. He did not have to convince me it was a good idea. We would be safer in there. Both your father and I hoped the captains might take us with them when they went upriver in the spring. Your father wanted to do it for the adventure, for the stories he would be able to tell, and for the money they would pay him. But my heart beat harder at one thought alone—*I might see my people and my home once again.*

❖

There was always much to watch at Fort Mandan. Every day the white men would tie their bright-colored cloth to a string and pull it to the top of a pole. They would stand together in lines and walk back and forth together in funny ways. This was called marching and drilling. Someday I will take you to where the soldiers do this here in St. Louis.

In the evenings they would sometimes make music. Pierre Cruzatte would play his fiddle, and the men would dance with one another. York was one of the best dancers of all.

No, Otter Woman and I did not dance. Nor did Jessaume's wife. We were married women, and the captains and the other white men always treated us with respect. Besides, there were so many young Mandan and Minnetaree women in the five villages, who admired the young white men. And the young white men admired them, too. Often those Americans would come back to the fort very late, after visiting some of those young women.

As soon as we moved into the fort, we began to work. The captains had great interest in Indian languages. Right from the start, their eyes would turn first to me. Unlike Otter Woman, I was not afraid to speak to them. I would tell them the words in Hidatsa. Charbonneau would then say those words in French. Then, if Jessaume was there, he and Jessaume would argue over which French word was the right one before translating it into English. At times Captain Lewis seemed ready to lose his temper with them both. But Clark would just laugh. Your father's ways have always amused him. It was easier when George Drouillard was there. He was good at French and English both, and never argued with Charbonneau. And you know how your father loves to argue.

❖❖❖

That winter began very cold. The snow fell early and deep and the river would soon freeze. It was not the time to leave the villages. But your uncle and the other Americans did not know that. Once again, word of trouble was brought to them. A raiding party of Arikaras and Sioux had attacked a group of Mandan hunters, killing one and stealing their horses. Four Minnetaree hunters from the upper village were missing, too. Perhaps the Sioux and Arikaras had killed them as well.

Immediately Captain Clark decided to pursue them. He called together twenty of the men and formed a war party. They went across the river to the Mandan village, seeking volunteers to help chase the Sioux. It would have been a crazy thing to do. Just walking through the snow-covered brush to the village had almost worn them out.

Captain Clark spoke to Big Man and Black Cat, the Mandan chiefs. "Come with us and help us punish the raiders," he said.

The chiefs shook their heads. They knew that revenge could wait until the spring, when the weather would be better. To go out now would be foolish.

"My father," Big Man said, "the snow is deep and it is cold. Our horses cannot travel through the plains now. Those people who spilled our blood have gone back."

So ended Captain Clark's war party. And as the snow got deeper and the weather grew colder, things became quiet in Fort Mandan. I continued to help as a translator, working almost every day. But the pace of life became slower. The Americans grew more relaxed. The Minnetarees and Mandans came and went freely, bringing food, sharing stories, playing games, and joking with the white men. Musicians came and danced and sang for the white men. In turn, the white men went to the villages, played their own music, and danced.

It was a time of sharing and making friends. People stared in wonder at the marvels the white men showed them. There was Captain Lewis's air gun, which made no explosion and used no gunpowder. There was the tube that made things far away leap up to you when you held it to your eye and looked through. There were many other Great Medicine objects made of metal and glass. When Captain Lewis saw my interest in his magical things, he seemed pleased and showed them to me, carefully explaining with words and gestures how they were used.

The white men had not brought enough food for the winter. Hunting grew more difficult with the snow. But there was much corn stored in the villages, and the captains traded for that corn. The worker of iron, John Shields, would repair hoes and firearms for people in exchange for corn. I sometimes stood to watch him as his hammer struck like a bolt of lightning and fire flew from the hot metal. I stood back, careful not to get in his way, but I knew I was welcome. Shields, like all of the men, always treated me with kindness and respect. It was not just that I was under the protection of the captains. I had become a part of their company. They treated me as a little sister.

Before long there were no more hoes needing repair. People asked for guns and powder in exchange for their corn. The captains refused. However, there was one weapon of war that they would trade. War axes. Shields began making war axes for trade. He cut apart an old iron stove to make them. For one battleax, he could get many baskets of corn in return. It was funny, was it not, Firstborn Son? The Americans told the Indians they were not allowed to fight any longer, and then they made battleaxes for them.

◄◆►

Three moons passed. Though the snow was still deep, the days were growing longer. Your motions inside my belly told me that you were restless. You wanted to start your own journey.

Your birth was not an easy one.

10

WILLIAM CLARK

Firstborn

11th February Monday 1805

about five Oclock this evening one of the wives of Charbono was delivered of a fine boy. it is worthy of remark that this was the first child the woman had boarn, and as is common in such cases her labour was tedious and the pain violent....

JOURNAL OF MERIWETHER LEWIS
FORT MANDAN, NORTH DAKOTA

NO, POMP, I WAS NOT THERE when you were born. But I remember it as clearly as if I were in the same room. Your mother and Charbonneau were living then in our quarters. We deemed it best for a young woman about to have her first child to be as close to us as possible. The best doctor for more than a thousand miles was Captain Lewis. Though Meri had not been trained as a medical man, he had studied hard for every possible problem along our way. Doctor Rush had prepared him well for every emergency. Already Captain Lewis had become famous as a physician among the Indians, who were always coming in for him to help them in some way to cure their ills. But I confess, lad, though he had foreseen flux and fevers, wounds and boils and pox, and the cutting off of frozen toes, none of us ever expected any of our little party to be giving birth.

Where was I? I was out with a hunting party. Our stock of meat was exhausted. With no meat in the camp and more than thirty hungry mouths, it mattered not that it was winter. I left, taking a good number of men with me. The first day, we walked more than thirty miles on the ice, and through points of land where the snow was more than knee-deep. And the hunting was not good. Even with twenty men to help me, we killed nothing on that first day. We were wet and hungry and we slept but little. The second day was both better and worse. I broke through the ice and got my feet and legs wet. But I sent four hunters through a point where I had seen the tracks of a deer. They killed a deer and two buffalo bulls. We butchered and ate that deer on the spot, but the buffalo were too meager to eat.

Though we did less well than we had hoped, we could not carry it all and had to cache a good stock of meat. So we came back for horses and sleds to bring the meat into camp. By the time I returned, the bottoms of my feet were blistered from walking on the uneven ice. All counted, we were out a full nine days.

Ah, your birth. Well, from what Meri told me it was not easy. That surprised me. I had fully expected you to come easily. Your mother had asked me to place my hand upon her belly so that I could feel you moving. Then she spoke with her hands. *He is ready to run*—I remember her saying. She was sure, by certain signs, that you were a boy. But her labor started in the morning and went all through the day with no sign that you were ready to deliver yourself into Meri's hands. Your mother asked for me, Meri said; she seemed to think that her son was waiting for my return. Even by then I had become the favorite in your mother Janey's eyes; the one she could rely upon.

"Out hunting," Captain Lewis said. "He will not be here."

Jessaume translated his words for her. Your father had absented himself from the room, troubled by your mother's pain.

"What can I do?" Meri said. He was not looking for an answer, but Jessaume had one.

"I have the remedy," Jessaume said. "If you have upon you the rattle of a snake."

Indeed, Meri did. As you know, Pomp, we were collecting specimens of every plant and new creature we saw along the way. Then the wise men of our people could see those things and learn. Among Meri's things was the rattle of a huge snake that had challenged him one day as we pulled in to the shore. Its challenge had lasted no longer than it took for Meri to end its career with his spontoon.

Jessaume took two rings from the rattle. He crushed them, mixed them into water, and gave them to your mother. As soon as she drank that potion, her pain eased. In less than ten minutes, you came into the world. Meri was much impressed and vowed to suggest that the doctors he knew conduct further experiments with this remedy when he returned to our homeland.

So it was that when I returned the next day from my long hunting trip, I found you waiting. You had been given the name of Jean Baptiste by your father. Your mother, Janey, in her own fashion and in her language, called you Pa-ump, Firstborn Son. And I called you Pomp.

11

SACAJAWEA

Charbonneau's Demands

Once there was a war among two of the bands of our people.
It began with a small quarrel, but it grew larger. Neither side
wished to give in, and many people died. At last the two
groups of warriors met on a high hill. They were about to
fight when a cloud of white smoke came swirling up toward
them.

"Look there below us," said the chief of the first band.

"It is a sign from the Great Mystery," said the chief of the
second band. "It means we should smoke the pipe of peace."

They went together to the place where the smoke rose from
a bubbling spring. They sat together and shared the pipe of
peace.

N O BABY COULD have been better than you. You hardly
cried, even that first night. You were hungry, though.
And when you were done eating, you yawned and went to
sleep. You held tight to one of my braids with your small hand
and slept. I was a woman of sixteen winters, and I was a
mother.

"He is very wrinkled," Otter Woman said. I knew she was teasing me because she was happy for me. I knew, too, that she wished she had a baby of her own to keep. Everyone knew that before two more moons passed we would be leaving the fort. You and your father and I would go up the river with the two captains to find the Great Salt Water. Otter Woman would not be able to come along. She would be left behind—just as the many young women in the five villages who had hoped to travel with us would be left behind. I would be the only one.

"He is very wrinkled," Otter Woman said again. Yes, she was jealous of us both.

I smiled up at her. "His wrinkles are beautiful," I said.

◆◇◆

Everyone came to see you. But it was not until our good captain came back from hunting that you smiled for the first time. You laughed, too. And when he reached his big finger down to touch your nose, you reached up and grasped his hand and would not let go. Then the two of you smiled and laughed together.

But we almost did not go on that great journey. Do you know why, Firstborn Son? Can you guess who it was who caused trouble? Think of how it is in our stories. Who is it who causes trouble when everything is going well for the people? Yes, Coyote is the one who does that. He is the one who does a good thing one moment and then a foolish thing the next, as if he cannot tell the difference between them. And who do we know like that? Yes, your father.

As I said, everyone knew we were to go with the captains. Everyone talked about it all the time. It was a great honor. It was exciting. It was the kind of journey that would give you stories you could tell for the rest of your lifetime. Wherever you went, people would ask you to tell those stories. The thought of the stories I could tell, though, meant less to me than going back home. I would be able to see the places I lived as a little girl. I would see the three rivers where I had been captured five winters before. Best of all, if they still lived, I might see some of my family again. I would be able to put my arms around them and hug them tight. That is our way, you know, Firstborn Son. More than any other nation, we Numi hug those we love and we hug those we meet. We hold them close so that our hearts are close together, so that our hearts are beating together.

Some were excited about our journey for other reasons. They were excited about what we could earn. Not just stories or honor, but land. Your father had heard that every man on the journey would be given the gift of a great piece of land. Each would receive the same grant of land that was given to the warriors who fought for the Americans in their great war against the British. That is how it is with the white people. They do not share their land with the other people in their nation. Each man holds his own piece of land and defends it as if it is the food on his plate and he is starving. It is strange, but that is how it is. Your father, Charbonneau, he is not like that. He likes the idea of having land, but he likes to travel even more. Now he talks of settling down here in St. Louis, but he will not. I know him. Soon enough he will want to go up the river again, to trap beaver, to visit different places, to hear the stories there. It is not easy, but it is always interesting to be around your father.

◆◆◆

People began to tell your father how important he was. The captains would not succeed without him. After all, his wife was the only one who could speak to the Snake Indians and help get horses. Without Snake horses, they would fail. Some of those who said these things to your father were jealous or worked for the English company. They hoped to cause trouble and make it more difficult for the captains to succeed. So your father did a foolish thing. He went to the captains and spoke to them in this way:

"The terms you offer me," he said, holding his arms wide open, "they are no good. I will not be your interpreter and bring my wife with me unless the terms are different. I will not stand a guard, *non*! And if I am miffed with any man, I must have the right to return as I please with as many provisions as I wish to carry. That is how my terms must be."

Then he folded his arms and waited for their agreement.

The two captains looked at each other with raised eyebrows but said nothing. Then they turned back to Charbonneau. Captain Lewis spoke.

"Your demands are inadmissible," Captain Lewis said. "Our engagement was only verbal. Monsieur Gravelines will be our interpreter. You may be off and take your family with you."

❖

The story of what had happened reached me before your father did. When he arrived I had already packed our things and I was walking toward the river with you in my arms. I said nothing to him. In fact, I said nothing to anyone except you, my son, the four days we spent in the Mandan village of Mitutanka, on the west bank of the frozen river. My silence troubled your father more than any complaints or angry words. When a man has been foolish, it is sometimes better to let him think of what he has done. If you tell him he is wrong, that just makes him more stubborn about it.

At first your father walked back and forth, waving his arms and complaining about the injustice of it. Was it not known that no one could translate as he, Toussaint Charbonneau, could? How could they speak to the many nations along the way without him? To interpret is great work, hard work. Why should they expect him to stay awake at night, keeping watch, when he needed to sleep so that he would be wide awake and ready to help them in the difficult job of translating? By the second day he was stating loudly that their journey would never succeed. It was better we did not go with them. They would all be killed by the Blackfeet or the Nez Percé. By the third day he was acting sad, asking why it was that the captains should dislike him so much—him, Toussaint Charbonneau, who only wished to be helpful to everyone. By the fourth day he was as silent as I was.

He sat for a long time, his chin in his hands, looking at the frozen river. Then he looked at me. Though I had spoken no word of criticism, he understood my silence. He came over to me, went down on one knee, and placed his hand gently on my shoulder.

"You wish to make this journey, is that not so, *ma petite*?" he said in a voice much smaller than usual.

"It is so," I said, surprised at how loud my own voice was in answering him.

"Then this foolish man shall do what he must do."

❖❖❖

Jessaume carried your father's words to the captains. Your father was sorry for the foolish part he had played. If the great captains Clark and Lewis pleased, he would accompany them, agreeable to the terms they had proposed. He would do everything they wished him to do. Would they excuse his simplicity and take him back into their service?

The next day we were called to return to Fort Mandan, where your father signed a written agreement and was officially enlisted as an interpreter.

12

WILLIAM CLARK

Departures

April 7th 1805

Sunday, at 4 oClock P.M, the Boat, in which was 6 soldiers 2 frenchmen & an Indian, all under the command of a corporal who had the charge of dispatches & c.——and a Canoe with 2 french men. Set out down the river for St. Louis. at the same time we sout out on our voyage up the river in 2 perogues and 6 canoes, and proceeded to the 1st villag. of Mandans & Camped on the S.S.——our party consisting of Sergt. Nathaniel Pryor Sgt. John Ordway Sgt. Pat: Gass, William Bratten, John Colter Joseph & Reubin Fields, John Shields George Gibson George Shannon, John Potts, John Collins, Jos: Whitehouse, Richard Windsor, Alexander Willard, Hugh Hall, Silas Gutrich, Robert Frazure, Peter Crouzat, John Baptiest la page, Francis Labich, Hugh McNeil, William Werner, Thomas P. Howard, Peter Wiser, J.P. Thompson and my Servent York, George Drewyer who acts as a hunter & interpreter, Shabonah and his Indian Squar to act as an Interpreter & interpretess for the Snake Indians——one Mandan & Shabonah's infant. Sah-kah-gar we a

THERE WAS NO DOUBT that spring was in the air, Pomp. Every day, even in the dead of winter, we had always had a steady stream—some days a flood—of Indian visitors. But then none at all came to the fort.

Why? we asked.

Because of the buffalo, Charbonneau said.

We went out to see. The ice had broken on the river, and the river had risen more than a foot in height. Here was a sight like no other. During the winter, when the buffalo herds crossed from one side to the other on the ice, betimes the ice broke, and many fell in to drown. Now their great frozen bodies were floating down the river. With extraordinary dexterity, the Indians were leaping from one small cake of ice to another, to catch those buffalo as they floated down.

The air was filled with smoke. Walking up to the rise on which the village stood, we looked in both directions and saw another sight. The Mandans had set fire to the grass on both sides of the river, and the whole prairie was ablaze. They did this every year, your mother told us through signs. It provided fresh grass for the horses and brought in the herds of buffalo.

Geese and ducks were flying up the river in huge flocks. We could hear them calling in the night. All our party was in high spirits. In a few days we would begin the next part of our great voyage.

◆◈◆

The day we chose to depart was Monday, April 7. At 4:00 P.M. we sent the keelboat back down the river. Your father and mother—and you, a baby held in your mother's arms—would be the only new additions to our Corps of Discovery. The three of you were with us that day on the riverbank as we watched the boat depart for St. Louis, carrying the only two of our original party who had not joined in our spirit of adventure: former privates Newman and Reed. Those two men, both much reformed; Corporal Warfington and four other privates; Mr. Gravelines, who served as both the river pilot and interpreter; and four Frenchmen made up the group that was going back to St. Louis. Captain Lewis had but little doubt that they would be attacked by the Sioux on their way down the river. But they pledged themselves, to a man, never to yield while there was a man of them living. They carried a critical cargo with them.

And what was in that cargo, Pomp? Our letters and reports, for one. And for another, nine boxes filled with wonderful things to be taken to the president of the United States. I have the list here. The skins and skeletons of such new creatures as the antelope, the mule deer, burrowing squirrels; the small burrowing wolf from the prairie—though its skin was lost by accident—horns of the mountain ram; a buffalo robe representing a battle between the Mandans and Minnetarees against the Sioux and the Arikaras; the skin of a yellow bear I obtained from the Sioux, a great bear of a sort we had yet to see; specimens of plants, insects, and mice; and cages containing a living burrowing squirrel of the prairies, four living magpies, and a living prairie hen. We had no doubt that such things would thrill President Jefferson, what with his great enthusiasm and curiosity for everything of a scientific sort.

◆◇◆

Were the rest of us fearful before we set out up the river? Perhaps we might have been. The unknown lay ahead of us. All contact with the civilized world would now be left far behind. Should disaster overtake us, we might vanish into that great unmapped wilderness without a trace. Yet all we felt was excitement. There was perfect harmony and good understanding among us. Such harmony and understanding I have never seen again in any group of men like our small party of adventurers. My dear friend Meri felt just as I did. We were about to voyage into the unknown.

He grasped me by the shoulder as we stood watching our men ready the boats for our departure. We looked at our little fleet of six small canoes and the two large pirogues.

"Billy," he said with a smile, "behold our little fleet."

"Not quite as respectable as Columbus," said I.

"Nor Captain Cook," Meri replied with a laugh. "Think of it. We are about to penetrate into a country two thousand miles wide, on which the foot of civilized man has never trodden. All the good or evil it has in store is for experiment yet to determine. Those little vessels of ours contain every article by which we are to expect to subsist or defend ourselves. Yet I do believe we shall succeed."

"And I believe the same," I said, my smile as broad as his.

◆◆◆

We took an early supper. That night we chose to sleep in a tent made in the Indian style, of the dressed skins of buffalo. Setting up the tent was your mother's responsibility, and she made it seem an easy one. I saw her do it many times in the months to come. The twelve poles raised and attached at the top in almost no time, other poles leaned in, the leather covering thrown over to make a cone. Inside that buffalo-skin lodge, your uncle Captain Lewis, George Drouillard, and I slept toward the front. At the back of the lodge, across the fire from us, were you, your father, and your mother. We were a little family within that lodge, and no man in our party ever showed anything less than perfect respect to your mother, though she was the only woman with us. Those sleeping arrangements were exactly as they would be for almost every night from then on until we reached the ocean.

The next day we set out very early. I was onboard the white pirogue, which carried our most precious things. In that white boat were our astronomical instruments, our best trade goods, our portable desks for writing, our medicines, much of our gunpowder, and all our journals and field notes. Six paddlers propelled us up the river. Yes, you and your father and your mother, Janey, rode with me in that very boat. Captain Lewis was so restless to be on the way that he felt the need for exercise and walked along the shore that first day—as he would in many of the days to come. He reached our first destination well ahead of us. He even had time to visit the Mandan village of Black Cat and smoke a farewell pipe with him.

We reached the point of land where he awaited us by noon. It had not been easy, for the wind had been hard against us. One of the small canoes had filled with water, ruining a quantity of biscuit and some thirty pounds of powder. This was a serious thing, though it proved our wisdom in packing the rest of our powder in tins that were watertight. Though there had been some difficulty, all in all that first day was a good one. We were on our way toward the undiscovered country.

13

SACAJAWEA

To Be of Use

Once a woman went out berry picking with her friends. She saw that a bear had been in the berry bushes before her. It made her angry.

"These bears are no good," she said. "They are smelly and stupid and they ruin our berry picking."

"Be careful," her sisters told her. "Do not speak of the Old One that way."

But that girl did not listen. She continued to insult the bear as she picked berries. After a while, because the bushes were so thick, her sisters could not hear her anymore. They became worried. They started to look for her, but she was gone. They looked and looked. At last they found her tracks and, next to them, the tracks of a huge bear. Her empty berry basket was there on the ground. She had been taken away by the One Who Walks Like a Man, and they knew they would never see her again.

DID I SHOW THEM THE WAY to go as we went up the Great Muddy River? No, Firstborn Son, how could I? Though I remembered well being stolen from my people at the Three Forks, those Minnetarees who took me did not come back to their village by boat. We came overland on horses. So after we passed the creek where your father had trapped beaver the year before, everything along the river was new to me.

But I was quick to show them how I could be of use to them, even before the time came for me to help them speak with our people. Their canoes and the two big boats were filled with wonderful things of all sorts. They carried with them provisions of different kinds, including salted meat and food that had been dried in preparation for a long journey. But they did not have enough food with them to feed more than twenty hungry mouths. They needed to hunt to survive.

The two captains were fine hunters. Drouillard was even better. I never saw a man who was better at tracking game or a finer shooter. No matter what the animal was, they would hunt it and bring it down—even if it was so far away from them it seemed that even a man with a gun would have no chance. In those first days of travel their talk was often of the animals they had been told about but had not yet seen.

They talked especially about the One Who Walks Like a Man. That is how our people always speak of the great bear, my son. If you do not show respect to the bear, he will not respect you. So it was that I worried when I heard the captains talk with excitement about hunting the grizzly bear. I hoped they would remember to respect him. They had many guns and they were great hunters, but even great hunters find it hard to kill the Old One.

In the meantime, they brought in elk and buffalo, deer and beaver. It seemed a plentiful hunt, even though some of the animals were still skinny and tough from the long winter. I knew, though, that the time would come when hunting would not be enough. High in the mountains, where our people live, animals would not be as numerous as they were in the lands we passed through at first. One day we would leave behind the great herds of buffalo. There would come a time when any animal would be hard to find. That was why, every fall, our Numi people would leave the safety of the mountains and go out on the plains to hunt the buffalo. Even though our enemies, the Blackfeet, might attack us there with their guns, we needed to hunt the buffalo and bring its meat back to our winter lodges. Without the buffalo hunt, we would not have had enough meat to survive until the spring run of salmon up the streams. Also, we women had learned long ago how to find food other than the animals the men hunt.

◈

I kept my eyes open. There is always the chance of attack by enemies when you travel out of your own land. Though the captains never seemed fearful of such dangers, I was. I had your safety to think about as well as my own. At any moment I might hear the whizzing song of the arrow in flight, followed by the thud of its point into human flesh and the cry of pain and despair of a wounded man that would follow. I knew those sounds well, having heard them at Three Forks on the day I was taken. Yet good fortune stayed by our sides. Day after day passed without even a single sign of an enemy.

I was watchful also for other things. On the second evening after we left the Mandan villages, I saw one of those things I had been looking for along the shore. There was a great pile of driftwood in a place where the earth seemed to be piled up on the bank of the river. I chose a strong driftwood stick of just the right size and began thrusting it into the soft earth. York walked with me, carrying a basket. He was often there, watching everything I did closely, as if hoping to learn enough so that he could live on this land as we do. I think our old friend York would be happiest if he were going up that great river again, as we did then.

Where were you then? Do you not remember? You were right there with me in your cradleboard.

Soon I broke through the roof of one of the granaries made by the harvester mice. It was stuffed with a great mound of the round white roots that are the size of a man's finger. Those roots have a sweet taste and the mice gather them in great numbers.

By then Captain Lewis was watching me also, with such care that I was certain he would make markings that night about what I had done. I had never seen men spend so much of their time making those markings in the little bundles of white leaves sewed together, which I later learned were called journals. Those journals, your good uncle explained to me, were as important to them as their own lives. Like the drawings on a winter count robe, the markings would help them and other men remember what they had seen and learned. It was strange to me, for I could see the pictures on a winter count robe clearly—the shapes of men and buffalo, of horses and lances. But all that I could see in the lines the two captains drew were shapes that made no sense to me. Yes, my wise son, I know that you are able to write such talking lines and understand what the talking lines made by others say to you. This is why your good uncle wishes you to stay with him. He wants you to know such powerful things as well as any white man.

I thanked the little harvester mice and gave them a present from my pouch. Then York and I filled the basket, making sure to leave some for the mice themselves, so that their own little ones would not starve. The captains and all the men were very pleased when they tasted those roots. Your father was as proud as if he had gathered those roots himself. He kept looking over at me and nodding. They ate all I had gathered and urged me to find more whenever I could. Then everyone sat around the fire, talking of that day's travel, and I sat with them. Captain Lewis's great dog, the one as large as a buffalo calf, came up and lay down beside me and then placed its head in my lap. I was happy that evening as I spread out our buffalo robe inside the tipi.

14

WILLIAM CLARK

Near Disasters

14th of May Tuesday 1805

A verry Clear Cold morning a white frost & some fog on the river the Thermomtr Stood at 33 above o, wind from the S.W. we proceeded on verry well until about 6 oClock a Squawl of wind Struck our Sale broad Side and turned the perogue nearly over, and in this Situation the Perogue filed with water....

JOURNAL OF WILLIAM CLARK
BROWN BEAR DEFEATED CREEK, MONTANA

SHALL I TELL YOU a bear story now? Ah, we had many adventures with the Old Hairy Ones, as your gentle mother calls them. She had warned me more than once, through signs and words, that they were dangerous, but neither I nor any man in our crew was willing to step back even one pace from danger. That is how young men are. We were more worried about encountering the hostile Assiniboines as we continued north toward the river's source. But fortune smiled on us, as she often did. In all our travels up the river to find the Shoshones we saw not a single Assiniboine. We would find their lodges by the river, their tracks, the rings where they had set up their tents, but not a single Indian.

At that time, with our concerns about hostiles, we worried not about bears. How could a few bears be of danger to us? After all, we had brought down the largest of buffalo with but a single shot. You see, we were just beginning to learn how much your mother truly knew.

Captain Lewis had been informed, before we set out from Fort Mandan, that the bear was like a great warrior, more frequent to attack a man than run from him. The Minnetarees told him that when they are about to hunt the bear they paint themselves and perform all the same superstitious rites as when they are about to make war upon a neighboring nation.

Our first difficulty, however, was neither bears nor hostile Indians. It was the wind. That wind never stopped blowing in our faces, carrying with it great quantities of fine sand from the sandbars in the river. Though we covered our noses and mouths, our eyes were sore. We had to eat, drink, and breathe sand. Even my pocket watch became filled with fine sand and stopped.

Then—April 24 it was—we feared we had lost one of our party. Captain Lewis's dog, Seaman, was gone the whole night and we feared he would not return. Meri was greatly satisfied when he reappeared the next morning. Fortunate it was that Seaman came back, for that great loyal dog would prove our savior more than once in the days ahead.

Five days later we took our first shots at two of those bears. Both were wounded. One escaped while the other attacked. It pursued Meri more than sixty yards. It was slowed by its wounds and we were able to fire again and dispatch it. We began to see why the Indians feared the bear so. But we remained confident that a weapon in the hand of a skilled rifleman made more than a match for the bear's ferocity.

On May 5 we killed another bear, the largest one yet. I am

sure the monster weighed more than six hundred pounds. From his nose to the extremity of his hind feet he measured eight feet, seven and one-half inches! Shot though he was through the lungs and in five other parts of his body, he still swam more than half the way across the river, roaring all the time.

By now the formidable appearance of these animals and the difficulty with which they died had staggered the resolution of most of our men.

"Meri," I said to Captain Lewis, "these bears being so hard to die rather intimidates me."

He nodded back to me, that look of concern on his face which always showed there when we was worried about the safety of our Corps of Discovery. "Billy," said he, "I must confess, I do not like the gentlemen. I had rather fight two Indians than one bear."

We quickly discovered that there were far more of those grizzly bears along the river than we had expected. In many places along the banks, the bodies of buffalo that had drowned in the winter and were rotting now had floated up. So the bears were coming down to feast upon them. We kept a close watch now. A single shot could not kill or even slow down a monster bear, the largest of them with backs so silvered that we began to refer to them as white bears. If one should encounter such a creature by oneself, those great teeth and long claws could do terrible damage. A man engaged in single combat with a bear would be lucky to escape with his life.

On May 14 we came close to disaster, in part because of those bears. It had been our practice always to have one of us in the white pirogue. Yes, that same boat in which you rode with your parents. Our most precious cargo was in that white pirogue. And I must tell you, Pomp, one of us had vowed always to stay in that boat because it also held your father. He had a great desire to be the one at the tiller, guiding the boat. Sad to say, but of all the watermen in the world, your father may be the worst and most timid. He had already almost tipped the boat over when he was at the helm one time before....Ah, has your mother told you about that?

◆◇◆

On that day, I was the one who chose to hunt along the shore. A great bear had been wounded and I thought I might see it. Though I did not know it at the time, the two rear canoes were then engaged in a fierce battle with that bear. It had lain in wait for them and charged out. It like to have defeated the whole party! Though they shot it many times, it still pursued them. Roaring, tearing at the brush with its jaws, it chased two of the men and almost caught them before they dived into the water. Then it leaped off a high bank into the cold river after them. There, as it floundered about, it was finally killed.

As fate would have it, while I was already onshore Captain Lewis felt an inclination to eat some veal. He, too, walked along the banks, where he killed a fine buffalo calf and a wolf with fur as white as the snowy wool of a sheep. Both Meri and I came back to the shore at the same time. We began to scan the wide river to see if we could find our little fleet.

"Billy," Captain Lewis cried out in a strangled voice, "look there!"

I looked and saw a scene three hundred yards distant that filled me with horror.

A squall of wind had struck the white pirogue and turned it sideways. It was close to turning topsy-turvy and it was filling with water. Worst of all, who was at the tiller but

Charbonneau, your father! But he was no longer holding the rudder. Instead, his hands raised to the sky, he was crying for mercy from his God. We shouted and fired our weapons to gain his attention, but we could not be heard, for he was on the river's far side. Meri actually began to strip off his clothing to swim out to the rescue, though he would not have gotten far in the waves and the icy water.

"Billy," Meri told me later that evening, a sad, serious look on his face, "I know my project was mad, but had the pirogue been lost I would have valued but little of my life."

But once again, Dame Fortune was with us. Two of those on board had not lost their heads while all the others were filled with fear for their lives.

Pierre Cruzatte, who was the bowman, picked up his rifle. He pointed it at Charbonneau and called out to him in French. *"Mon ami,"* he shouted, "if you do not take the rudder and straighten this boat, I will shoot you."

Heeding Cruzatte's repeated threats, Charbonneau took the rudder and straightened the boat. Though it was near filled with water, two hands bailed and two others paddled, and they brought it in safely to shore.

At the same time, your good mother was reaching out and pulling back into the boat all of those things that were floating away. Were it not for her quick actions and clear thought, we would have lost much that was priceless. No one on board had more fortitude and resolution than our Janey!

15

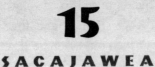

SACAJAWEA

Difficulties

*Long ago, there was a Great Sea in the land of our people.
Our people would fish from its shores for food. But the fish
decided that they would not allow our people to catch them.
Our people became thin and hungry.*

*They prayed for help. "Creator," they prayed, "it is not
right that the fish should not allow themselves to be caught.
Was this world not made so that all of its beings could
survive? Now we are suffering. We need your help."*

*That is when the Creator took pity on our people. The
waters of the Great Sea began to shrink. The sea grew smaller
and smaller, leaving the fish in shallow pools where our people
could catch them. Our people were able to get plenty to eat,
and they dried more fish to keep for the future.*

*Finally the sea was gone. All that was left was a river
that flowed through the mountains. It was full of fish, and
because it was so much smaller than the sea, it was not hard
for our people to catch them. So it is to this day.*

A ND NOW YOU ARE READY to hear more of the story of our travels, Firstborn Son? You are certain you have done all that you were told to do and not spent the morning playing with our good captain's dogs?...

Yes, those dogs are wonderful, almost as wise as a person. But the wisest and best dog I ever knew was with us on our journey. He was the friend of Captain Lewis. Yes, Seaman. And I have told you before that he was the size of a buffalo calf, but as gentle to us as a mother to a child, have I not? When he slept, it was always at the door of our lodge, guarding us from harm.

So it was on the night when he saved us all. He had been injured a few days earlier. A beaver that he caught in the river had bitten him so hard that he bled and bled and the captains thought he would die. Even though he was still limping, he was back at his familiar place, keeping guard.

That night, not long after your father almost sank the big white canoe, we were wakened by Seaman's barking outside the tipi. As I sat up, holding you close to me, I heard the shouting of men, the thudding of heavy feet on the ground coming closer, and the chuffing sound that could only be the heavy breathing of some great animal. The men rushed outside. Looking out through the tent flap after them, I saw such a sight! A huge bull buffalo was rushing, head down, right for us. But, still growling and barking, Seaman placed himself in the way of the buffalo and turned it aside just before it ran into us. It passed so close that its shoulder brushed the tent, and then it vanished into the night.

The next morning we saw the tracks where it had come out of the river. It had climbed right over the big white boat, stepping into it as it went and badly damaging the rifle that belonged to York. Captain Clark spoke hard words to him about leaving his weapon in the boat, and York was unhappy all through that day. Captain Lewis kept walking around the white boat, speaking to himself and shaking his head.

"What is he saying?" I asked your father.

"He thinks that the big white boat has a bad spirit with it," Charbonneau said. "And he is right. This devil boat has already tried to kill me twice."

But I could not agree. Though the buffalo had run through our camp, its feet striking the earth right next to the heads of the sleeping men, no one had been injured. All that was hurt was the gun, and the blacksmith would soon fix that. It seemed to me as if good spirits were with the two captains, protecting them along their way. As difficult as our journey would be, I was certain those good spirits would help us succeed.

Soon we passed the River That Scolds All Others. That is how the Indians call it. But the captains gave it a different name. They called it the Milk River. That was something they did everywhere, Firstborn Son. Even though we came to places that already had names, they gave those places new names. It would have been hard for them to remember those new names, had they not made their marks on the white leaves.

Just after we passed the wide river the Minnetarees call the Musselshell, we came to a smaller river, one that flowed strong with clear water. The two captains both looked at me that day as they made marks in their books. That river, they told me, now shared my name. It was now Bird Woman's River. I felt something then. I still cannot tell you whether I was proud, but I was touched that they had done this. It was strange to leave a part of myself with that river.

We came now to a country where the Minnetarees never traveled. They always cut across the plain on horses after the River That Scolds All Others. But with our boats, we had to stay in the water. I was glad to not be on the shore. There was great danger there. There were more dead buffalo along the river's banks, and even more bears. When he was out with Drouillard, your father was almost caught by one of those bears.

"I will be the one to kill this bear," Charbonneau said to Drouillard. But when it charged at him, your father fired his gun into the air and ran. *"Mon Dieu,"* your father shouted, "have mercy on me!"

While the bear tried to find him, your father hid in the bushes. At last Drouillard was able to shoot the bear in the head and kill it.

All along the river great white cliffs rose. The rocks lifted up in strange, beautiful shapes. I thought they looked like the lodges of powerful beings. It seemed to me as if there were many stories in those stones. The river was twisting now like a snake, and there were stones everywhere. The men had to climb out and pull the boats with ropes, and the ropes kept breaking. As before, the big white boat was the one that caused the most trouble. It was as if that place did not wish us to pass through. Perhaps it was the medicine of that place that made me become ill. I told your father that I was not feeling well, that a pain was growing in my stomach. He ignored me. He was trying hard not to attract the attention of the captains for fear they would make him climb out of the big white boat and pull on those ropes.

The captains were excited, despite the difficulty of the river. They had finally seen the tallest mountains, where our Numi people live. Soon they would come to the Great Falls, and then the mountains would be close. So the Minnetarees had assured them. But then something happened. The river that had been one stream became two. Two rivers flowed together to become the Great Muddy. Which of them came from the Great Falls?

I could not help them. I had never been to this place before.

"I do not know which river is the one to follow," I said, and your father translated my words. Then I clutched my stomach. The pain was growing worse.

Captain Clark looked at me with concern.

"It is nothing," your father said, trying to convince himself as much as the captains. "It is a woman's illness. *Ma petite* Bird Woman, she will be well soon."

I waved them away from me, not wanting to add to their troubles. Then, though Captain Clark continued to glance over at me, the discussion went on. Everyone talked long and hard. Scouting parties were sent up both rivers. At last almost everyone was certain. The Missouri was the deeper, swifter river, the muddy one that came from the north. Only two people disagreed. Those two were Captain Clark and Captain Lewis. The bed of the river to the west was made of stones, like that of a river coming from the mountains. So that was the river that came from the Great Falls. Everyone was sure they were wrong. But because they were the captains, everyone agreed to follow them.

Once again the good spirits were with our captains. The

river from the west was the right one. Captain Lewis scouted ahead. After only a few days he came to the Great Falls. But he saw that there was still much difficulty ahead. For there was not just one set of falls, but many. The boats and all their things would have to be taken across the rocky land filled with cactus until the river ran smooth again, above the many falls. It would be a hard, hard journey of many days.

He hurried back to tell the others of his discovery. While he was gone, I had grown sicker. Though Captain Clark tried to release the spirits of my sickness from my body by cutting my legs and making me bleed, nothing had helped. My arms and hands trembled, my eyes saw only darkness. I was certain that I would soon die.

16

WILLIAM CLARK

The Great Falls

June 16th of Sunday 1805

*the wind roared from the S.W. hard and Some rain at about
2 oClock Capt Lewis joined me from the falls 5 miles distant
& infd. that the Lard Side was the best portage I despatched
2 men on the Lard. Side to examine the portage.—the
Indian woman verry bad, & will take no medisin what ever,
untill her husband finding her out of her Senses, easyly
provailed on her to take medison, if She dies it will be the
fault of the husband as I am now convinced—.*

JOURNAL OF WILLIAM CLARK
GREAT FALLS, MONTANA

I FEAR THAT I did little good helping your mother when
she was ill, Pomp. Though each of us on our great voyage
of discovery had to know something of doctoring, I was better
at such things as the mending of broken bones or the sewing
up of a wound. When it came to real illness, it was Captain
Lewis who served as our physician. And no doctor could ever
have cared better for a patient than Meri did for our Janey. As
soon as he returned from the Great Falls he rushed to her. I
told him what I had done as he checked her pulse and found it
scarcely perceptible. Charbonneau hovered over him, wringing

his hands. Neglectful as he might have been of your mother before her condition became so grave, your father never left her side all the time she was ill, and he would eat or drink nothing until she was well.

Captain Lewis lowered his head in thought, it seemed, biting his lower lip as he did so. Though it could have been no more than a minute or two, it seemed an eternity to your father and me. At that moment I was certain he would raise his head, shake it, and say that there was no hope. But in those days Captain Meriwether Lewis was not a man to give in to his despair, not while there was still a continent to cross. He looked over at Charbonneau and me and nodded his head with that old certainty of his.

"Billy," he said, "remember the sulfur spring we found on the other side of the river? Its water in all appearance is precisely similar to that of Bowyer's Spring in Virginia. I'm resolved that we must try its virtue on her."

Then he sent a man to bring back some of that water while I helped make ready for the great portage we would soon begin. In the meantime he began giving her doses of Peruvian bark and laudanum. Slowly her pulse became steadier and stronger. All through that day he continued to treat her. He made her drink the water of the spring and gave her more of his medicines. By that evening a gentle perspiration had come on and her illness much abated. By the next day she was free of pain, clear of fever, and eating as freely as Meri would permit her of broiled buffalo well seasoned with pepper and salt. He had brought her back almost from the dead.

"You have done a fine thing, Meri," I said to him.

"What else could I do?" he answered. "She being our only dependence for a friendly negotiation with the Snake Indians."

And that was how Captain Lewis was, practical and clear minded. But I knew that he was almost as fond as I of your mother and you. Yes, and even of your father, old Charbonneau, with his thousand faults. The health and well-being of your little family meant almost as much to us by then as did our success in the great endeavor.

During Meri's doctoring of your mother, I was overseeing all else that had to be done. We had already hidden the larger of our two boats, the red one, and continued toward the Great Falls in the white pirogue, despite its many misfortunes. Cruzatte had showed us how to make a cache, and in it we stored quantities of food and gunpowder and other supplies we would need on our return journey. Now we saw that we must also leave the white pirogue behind. We hid it in the middle of a small island in the north fork. Our portage of more than twelve miles around the falls and rapids would be arduous. We had to travel as light as we could and yet take with us all that was needed.

One of the things, indeed the heaviest, was the bulky framework of an iron boat that Captain Lewis was fond of. That boat was, I must admit, the oldest of his companions on the journey. It had been with him long before I was. He had invented it himself and brought it all the way from Harper's Ferry. Our men referred to it as the Experiment, and had lugged it without complaint, even though the general thought was that it would fail. Without a word, your mother had summed up the opinion of all save Captain Lewis. Upon being told what the heavy metal frame was for, she reached out a hand to touch a large rock, pointed at the river and then let her hand fall quickly, as if sinking like a stone.

Captain Lewis, though, had no doubts. When we reached the other side of our portage, we would assemble the frame of the boat, cover it with the twenty-eight elk skins and two buffalo skins we had prepared, caulk it with pine pitch, and then float away. Or so Meri expected. While we did the portage he would ready his miraculous vessel.

"My boat," he said "will easily hold eight thousand pounds, and when unloaded can be carried by only eight men with the greatest of ease."

Eight men, I thought. And I resolved to keep my eyes open for groves of cottonwood trees that could be made into dugout canoes when the great boat experiment failed.

The distance was too far for us to carry everything on our shoulders. We made four sets of truck wheels from the only cottonwood tree in sight within twenty miles. The mast of the white pirogue was cut down and sawed into axles. With coupling, tongues, and bodies, we could use those wheels to draw our canoes and baggage along on the portage. I went and surveyed the route we would take. At last, just after sunrise on June 22, we began the portage. By then your mother was quite recovered. She was walking about and fishing in the river!

That ten-day portage around the Great Falls was the hardest we made. The prickly pears stuck our feet through our moccasins. The axle trees and tongues of our wheels broke down as they followed the route I had staked out. So many buffalo had trodden the earth that it was uneven and worse than frozen ground. The men had to catch at grass and knobs and stones to draw the canoes and loads. The mosquitoes were extremely troublesome, as were large black gnats that did not sting but swarmed about us and filled our eyes.

Your mother kept your head covered with her blanket to protect your eyes, but her own were never closed. She was constantly on watch and warning us of danger, which was there in plenty. The great white bears were now more numerous than ever before. They followed us as we pulled our loads, coming so close we thought they would surely attack. They were so many that we did not dare to send one man alone out on any errand, particularly if he had to pass through the brush. Each night the bears would come around our camp. Captain Lewis's great dog, Seaman, was awake all through those nights. Patrolling back and forth, he gave us timely notice of the bears' visits. Had he not been there, the white bears surely would have ventured to attack. It seemed that there was no end of difficulty and danger to be had as we struggled our way toward the White Bear Islands camp, where Meri was now engaged in the long task of assembling the Experiment.

It was near the end of that hard portage, on Saturday, June 29, that a series of sudden heavy rains began to fall. Those rains, my lad, almost ended your life.

17

SACAJAWEA

Flash Flood

Long ago, a man and his wife were fishing in the river. He had waded deep into the water, using his spear to catch fish. Each time he speared a fish he would throw it back to his wife on the shore, and she would place it into her basket. But then as that man thrust at a large fish, he lost his footing and fell into the swift current. As it swept him away, his wife jumped into the deep water after him. She pushed him toward shore, and he was able to climb out of the water. But when he turned to pull his wife out, she was gone. She had given her life to save him.

That man was sick for a long time. He did not know if he wanted to keep on living. But when he was well enough to return at last to that river, a shape lifted up in the mist near the falls. It was the spirit of his wife.

"Do not be sad," his wife's spirit said. "I will always be here to warn my people of the danger. Now I will always be able to help others. I am happy here."

You want to hear about the day of the flood? How your good uncle saved our lives? It was a few more than two handfuls of days after Captain Lewis saved my life with his medicine. I felt so well that I was able to accompany your father and your good uncle as they walked along the trail that we had to take to get around the many falls. In fact, I think your good uncle wanted me to be with them. It seemed as if he was always watching over me, in much the same way as I watched over you, Firstborn Son.

The strong winds and rains had come, those winds and rains that come to our land during the Moons of Long Days. That morning the ground was so wet from one such rain that the men were not able to push the boats on wheels any farther. Captain Clark had lost some of the talking leaves on which he had made marks about the path they were to travel. So he decided to walk back that way, along the river between two of the waterfalls. York, your father, and I—and you, in your cradleboard—were the only ones with him.

As we walked along a deep ravine, York saw buffalo in the distance. He looked over at your good uncle.

Captain Clark smiled. He knew how much York loved to hunt. "Go ahead," he said. "It would be good to have the hump and tongue of a fat buffalo."

We walked on only a little way farther before the wind came. It howled around the stones like a great wolf, and it almost knocked us down upon the ground. With it came the drumbeat of hail. The hail had not reached us yet, but we could see it coming across the green earth of the plain. The hail was striking with such force that it tore up the earth as it came. Your father, Charbonneau, did as he usually does when threatened by danger. He stared at the hailstorm as it thudded closer.

Your good uncle saw what danger we were in. The wind was so strong that it might throw us from the cliff and into the river. The balls of hail were as large as my fists, big enough to injure or even kill a person. We had to find shelter.

"There!" Captain Clark shouted over the howling of the wind, pointing at a shelving rock near the bottom of the ravine.

He cradled his rifle in his arm as he pushed me ahead of him with his elbow. I held your cradleboard tight and reached out my other hand to grasp your father's sleeve, pulling him with us as we scrambled down the slope.

There, on the upper side of the ravine, the ledge of stone sheltered us well from the wind. The hail rattled over us, great balls of ice exploding onto the stones of the ravine. But we stayed safe and dry beneath the shelf of stone. I loosened you from your cradleboard and held you close to me. Captain Clark and your father placed their guns, their powder horns, and their other things down by their sides as they sat. To keep himself busy, your father started to clean his gun with the wiping rod he had borrowed earlier that day from Captain Lewis.

The rain was still falling, but the rattling of the hail had ended. Your good uncle and your father were enjoying being safe from the power of the storm. But I was worried. Something was not right. A deeper sound, like the growling of a great, distant bear, was making itself heard.

"Listen!" I shouted as I reached out to shake your good uncle's shoulder. He peered out from our shelter to look up the ravine. We both saw it coming toward us. It was a flash flood.

Great boulders were being pushed in front of it as if they were birds' eggs. If the flood struck us it would carry us downstream to sweep us over the Great Falls. There we would surely be killed, if we were not first drowned.

Your good uncle did not hesitate. As always, he knew just what to do. He pushed your father out of our shelter ahead of him. He grabbed his rifle and shot pouch with his left hand and thrust me up the loose stones of the slope with his other hand. I had no time to put you back into your cradleboard. I just held you tight as Captain Clark tried to save our lives from the flood. The rushing waters had already risen up to his waist, pulling at him as a mountain lion pulls at the haunches of a deer struggling to escape.

And what did your father do then? Can you not guess? He froze. His feet forgot how to walk. He held tight to my hand, wanting to help us, but he was not moving. Captain Clark kept pushing me with his right hand and prodding your father with the barrel of his rifle as we climbed. By the time we reached the top, the ravine had become filled with water that growled at us, angry because we had escaped its quick hunger.

◆◇◆

York found us at the top of the ravine. Seeing the storm strike, he had stopped hunting and dashed back to find us. We were wet and cold, bruised by the stones of the ravine. Captain Clark had given the flood his big compass and his moccasins. Both he and your father had their tomahawks and powder horns taken from them. Charbonneau had also lost Captain Lewis's wiping rod. Your cradleboard and all your clothing now belonged to the river. But we were alive.

York had with him a canteen filled with the water that warms you. Your good uncle had me drink some of it. But he did not let us rest. You were naked and I had just recovered from my illness. He was afraid that both of us would become sick. He gave up any idea of going farther.

"York," he said, "move them to our camp on the run."

Then he hurried on ahead of us. When he reached the camp, he found everything in confusion. We were not the only ones who had suffered. The hungry storm that had tried to steal our lives had struck the men while they were out on the plains. They had dropped their loads and run. The wind was like a great hand, slapping them down. The wall of hail had hit them so hard that it knocked them off their feet again and again as they ran. They were much bruised and bleeding. It had been a day that I would never allow myself to forget.

18

WILLIAM CLARK

◆◆◆◆◆◆◆◆◆◆◆◆◆◆◆◆◆◆◆◆◆◆

The Three Forks

July 9th Tuesday 1805

on trial found the leather boat would not answer without the addition of Tar which we had none of, Substituted Cole & Tallow in its place to Stop the Seams &c. which would not answer as it Seperated from the Skins when exposed to the water and left the Skins naked & Seams exposed to the water. this falire of our favourate boat was a great disapointment to us, we haveing more baggage than our Canoes could Carry. Concluded to build Canoes for the Carry them; no timber near our Camp. I deturmined to proceed on up the river to a bottom in which our hunters reported was large Trees &c.

JOURNAL OF WILLIAM CLARK
ABOVE THE GREAT FALLS, MONTANA

I WILL CONFESS, Pomp, that it was with a good bit of uncertainty that we dropped the Experiment into the river that day. To my surprise, it floated like a perfect cork.

Meri was as happy as a little child with an extra serving of pudding. He had worked for days to find something to fill in the seams of the boat. Pine pitch would have been the best. But there were no pine trees within a four-day journey of us. The other men and I had scouted the land there at the end of the long portage. I had walked twenty or thirty miles a day, through rocks and brush and prickly pears, wiping gnats out of my eyes and enduring the hum of the mosquitoes in my ears. There were no pines. So Meri had made up a "composition," as he called it. It was a mixture of charcoal and tallow and he covered the boat with two coats of it, drying it over a fire.

Seats were fixed into it and oars made ready. But then one of those sudden winds struck again, and we had to wait until its violence blew over. When we came back to the water, we found that Meri's "composition" had begun to peel off in great flakes. His favorite boat was half filled with water. We pulled it from the river. The seams had come open. There was no way it could be repaired.

The look on Meri's face was sad to behold. He had brought the Experiment three quarters of the way across the continent, only to have it fail just when it was most needed. No one said a word.

Meri ran his hand along the skins of the boat. "See here, where the hair was left on the buffalo skins?" he said in a soft voice. "It answered much the best purpose here. Had I but singed the elk skins instead of scraping them, or used only buffalo skins, she would have answered our need." Then he shook his head. *"Adieu,"* he said.

He helped the men pull the boat from the river. With six men, he stripped the skins off and placed the frame of our failed Experiment into the hole that had been dug to hold the tar. Then, with nothing further to do, he went off to fish in the river.

In the meantime I had set off with a crew of five men to a small grove of cottonwoods that had been sighted by our hunters eight land miles upriver. There we found just two trees. They were wind shaken but would serve. Both were three feet across. One was twenty-five feet long and the other thirty-three. During the five days it took to hollow them out, Meri supervised the carrying of all our baggage to the cottonwood grove where we were working.

◆◆◆

Have you ever heard the voice of the mountains, Pomp? We heard it first during those days at the end of the portage, just before we set out again on the river. The Minnetarees had told us about it before we set out, and your mother had agreed that there was such a thing.

"Wait," she said. "You will hear their strong voice."

I was beginning to understand by then that when your mother, Janey, said something was so, that was just how it was. But Captain Lewis had paid no attention, thinking it false.

"The phantom of a superstitious imagination," he said.

Then we heard it. It was like thunder or the firing of a big gun—a great cracking sound that came rolling over the plain. It wasn't at regular intervals, but only now and then. Sometimes in the morning, sometimes just before the sunset, and always from the same direction. "The artillery of the Rocky Mountains" is what we began to call it. Hearing it reminded us again of how many strange and wonderful things were all around us. It also reminded us how far we were from home.

◆◆◆

But you are right, my boy. Not all of us were far from home. We were coming closer to your mother's own homeland, and we were in hopes of soon seeing her people, the Snakes. We did not know, at first, how unlikely that was at that time of year. Because of the Blackfeet, her people were staying in the mountains, even though there was little to eat. I

102

saw this for myself when we found an abandoned old camp of her people's with some of their little houses of woven brush. Your mother showed me the peeled pine trees.

"This is how we do it to collect the sap and pith for food," she explained.

But though we did find signs of a recent large encampment of Blackfeet Indians, we found no recent camps of her Snake people.

We learned later that they would only make their great foray onto the plains at the end of the summer, to hunt the buffalo whose meat would help them survive another winter. Since the Snakes lacked the guns that their enemies had obtained freely from the English, their buffalo hunt had to be like a raid into enemy territory, short and swift. They had to be ready to flee at any moment. Only small bands would come onto the plains before the great buffalo raid. Few, if any, of Janey's people would be seen here near the river. And if they were to see us, they would likely run from us in fear.

◆◆◆

Hard as the land was, it was beautiful. The sunflowers were everywhere, as yellow as that ball of light in the sky. There was a great abundance of ripe serviceberries and currants, red and black, purple and yellow. Even the prickly pears, terrible as they were to walk among, were in bloom all around us. Those thorns were so keen and stiff they would pierce the double thickness of a dressed deerskin with ease. One evening after I had walked thirty miles, we camped by the light of the fire. I pulled seventeen of those briars out of my feet. Meri, practical as he always was, suffered less than I did. He had taken the trouble to sew an extra sole of buffalo hide onto his moccasins.

It was July 20 when I saw my first clear sign of your mother's people, the Snakes. But it was not a hopeful sign. We had just killed an elk when we saw a great cloud of smoke rising from the little valley above us, where a large creek flowed into the river. It appeared that the country up the valley of the creek, which we later named Smoke Creek, had been set on fire.

When I told your mother of it, she explained it to me.

"It is a signal to run away," she said.

Hearing the shots of our guns, the Snakes had thought we were a war party of their enemies and set the fire to warn the others. They then fled from us over the mountains. I left behind pieces of cloth to show that we were friends, but my heart was low. If the Snake people feared us so much, how could we ever come close enough to show that we were friends?

19

SACAJAWEA

What Do You Call Us?

Long ago, many of our people were sick. So our chiefs called on a medicine man to help them. His name was Man from the Sky. He went into his lodge, opened his medicine bundle, and prayed. When he was done, he told the people to bring all those who were sick to him. He would take them on a journey. He led the people up the Snake River to a place in the hills. Then he went up the hill and tapped a rock with his stick. Healing water flowed from that rock. The people bathed in that water and grew well again.

Y OUR GOOD UNCLE had made himself ill. With all of his walking through the prickly pear cactus, his feet were covered with open wounds and blisters. He was so tired that it was an effort for him to stand again after he sat upon the ground. Yet he did not wish to stop. His heart told him to keep seeking my people, even after Captain Lewis begged him to rest.

Although we had not yet found my relatives, we had come to the lands that I remembered. They were as clear in the eye of my heart as if I had slept but a single night without seeing them, even though it had been five winters. My heart pounded and it seemed as if it would burst from my chest when I first recognized a place where the river bent around a little island filled with wild onions.

But I could not tell if I was filled with happiness at returning home or if my heart was beating so fast because I was afraid of what I might find. What had happened to those close to my heart when the Minnetarees raided on that harsh day? Were any of them still alive? Was my mother among the living? My brother, Stays Here? What of my friends? Would I ever again see the face of anyone from my childhood other than Otter Woman?

It had been many moons since I had seen Otter Woman. It was so long now since those nights in the Minnetaree village where we had sat with our heads close together, speaking to each other in our own language. Our language is one that your father has never learned or wished to learn.

There were so many questions in my mind, so many voices speaking to me from within, I could not answer them all.

So I showed no emotion, for I did not know what emotion it was that now made my whole body tremble as it did.

"This is the river on which my relations live," I told them. My voice stayed calm. "The Three Forks are no great distance from here."

All of them were made happy by my words. Though he was ill, your good uncle hugged me, and Captain Lewis looked at me with a brief smile and nodded his head.

Such a serious man, Captain Lewis was. It always seemed as if there was something that made him doubt himself, even though he was good and strong. It is not that way with your good uncle. He always knows who he is. The red of his hair is a sign of the sunshine that lives in his heart. The spirit power in his heart is his friend. It never confuses him.

Now I could tell them where we were going and help show them the way. The captains were so pleased that they gave me a beautiful string of the blue beads that everyone loves. I used them as a belt. I did not own that belt long, but I still remember how good it felt to my touch, how proud I was to be useful. Now I was not just the one who set up the tent, who found the good roots to eat. I was also the one who could show them the way to my people, the one who could help them get horses.

Yes, Firstborn Son, your good uncle told you they expected this of me all along. But perhaps their hopes would not have come true. I might have been like that iron boat, unable to carry the load. Now it seemed all they hoped of me would come true. My heart was singing.

But we still had not met with my people.

❖

As we went along I showed them things. There was the creek where we got the earth from which we made our white paint. I taught them how a friend would paint the cheeks of someone he or she met. I told them that they should carry paint with them. If they ever met any of my people, they should use the vermilion paint to honor them in this way. I explained how we would greet friends. You know how it is done, Firstborn Son. We put the arms closest to our hearts around each other's shoulders, we press our cheeks together like this. And what do we say? Uh-huh. We say *"Ah-hi-e, ah-hi-e." I am so pleased, I am so pleased.*

They listened closely to me and nodded. But Captain Lewis needed to know something else. Captain Lewis was trying to find words to speak in other languages. Though he sometimes got them wrong, as soon as he was able to turn them into his marks on white leaves he was sure he understood perfectly.

"What do you call us?" Captain Lewis asked.

"You are the Red-Haired Captains," I answered.

"No," he said, looking unhappy. "That is not what I mean," he said, speaking very slowly, as if it were his words, not his question, that had confused me. "All of us." He gestured with his hands. Then he looked at our little party. He motioned for York to take Seaman and lead him off to the side. He had your father join them. Then he made a circling motion, including him, your good uncle, and the other men who came from far away. "All of *us*," he said.

He wanted our word for white men. But I still could not understand. Your father looked worried. Captain Clark caught my eye. He held out one of his hands and raised an eyebrow.

"Janey?" he said.

I had to say something or Captain Lewis would have been unhappy all that day. I remained silent, though, until Captain Lewis asked one more question. He made the motion in sign language that stands for our people.

"What would your people, the Snakes, call us?"

At last I thought I understood. *"Ta-ba-bone,"* I said. *"Ta-ba-bone."* It is a word for those who are strangers, who might be enemies.

"Ta-ba-bone," Captain Lewis said. He was very pleased. He smiled as he turned it into black lines on a white leaf. *"Ta-ba-bone."*

Despite his sickness, your good uncle kept scouting ahead, walking far along the shore and farther inland as we came down the river in the cottonwood canoes. Your father had sprained his ankle some days before, but he assured Captain Clark he was better now. He begged to go with him. You know how your father always wants to see something new. So your good uncle agreed. And I remained behind.

<hr>

The mountains were so close to the river now that we could no longer see the ranges of peaks beyond them. Captain Lewis was greatly worried that we would come to waterfalls or dangerous rapids.

"No," I told him, "our river has no such places. It flows all the way just as it does now."

He did not believe me, or at least he was not ready to let go of his worries. He was troubled so much by the insects that bit him. His eyes and face were always swollen, even though he covered his head each night with the thin cloth you can see through. He also kept urging your good uncle to cease his walking and allow him to take a turn looking for our people. But everyone in our party, including Captain Lewis, knew that your good uncle was the better of the two men at speaking with Indians. You could see in his face how he enjoyed meeting our people, sharing their food, and hearing their stories. Captain Lewis only showed such excitement when he looked at some small plant he had never seen before or when an animal or bird new to him was brought in. Then he would spend much time making his marks on the white leaves, sometimes even drawing the exact shape of that fish or animal or bird.

<hr>

It was a fine day when we came to the place where I had been taken captive. There were the Three Forks of the river, that same river I had spoken to on that day long ago when I made my foolish wish to travel. The river had certainly heard me then. I whispered to it again.

"Help my friends," I said in a very soft voice. Then I stood quietly on the banks and looked.

Now your good uncle was so sick that he had no wish to eat. Yet he wanted to walk. He walked along the north branch of the three rivers with only your father and one other man by his side.

The river almost took your father that day, Firstborn Son. They were wading together out to a large island when your father lost his footing. He was pulled into the deep water by the fast current. Weak though he was, your good uncle came into the river after him and pulled him to safety. Then they continued on to the island, where Captain Clark decided to camp for the night. His scout for my people had not succeeded.

20

WILLIAM CLARK

Finding the Shoshones

Thursday August 8th. 1805.

the Indian woman recognized the point of a high plain to our right which she informed us was not very distant from the summer retreat of her nation on a river beyond the mountain which runs to the west. this hill she says her nation calls the beaver's head from a conceived resemblance of it's figure to the head of that animal. she assures us that we shall either find her people on this river or on the river immediately west of it's source; which from it's present size cannot be very distant.

JOURNAL OF MERIWETHER LEWIS
SOUTH OF HELENA, MONTANA

IT WAS NO EASY JOB to find your mother's people, Pomp. By the time the month of August began, I had walked so many miles that my feet felt like a worn-out pair of moccasins and there was a swelling on my ankle, just here, almost the size of one of your little fists. But the men in our little fleet of canoes were no less worn and weary than me. The river had grown shallower and swifter, and we had to push our way with poles or climb out into the water and pull our boats along. All of us were blistered and bruised, stabbed by cactus, and bitten by insects.

Our "trio of pests" was what Meri called the mosquitoes, gnats, and prickly pears together. "Billy," he said to me, "they are equal to any three curses that ever poor Egypt labored under!" And he spat out a mouthful of gnats at the end of his words as a punctuation mark.

◆◆

He and I had agreed that if my own scout for the Shoshones should not have succeeded by the end of July, then Meri would be the one to try to find their trail. So I took his place among the boats and watched as he set out up the mountain slope. Your father, Charbonneau, Drouillard, and Sergeant Gass went with him. Though they were gone near a week, they found not even a single Indian. And your father had a devil of a time keeping up with Lewis and the others, complaining about his sore feet. In the meantime I had gone out to kill a deer and found a man's tracks along the river. From the look of them, they were the prints of an Indian. He had seen or heard us coming and made a quick retreat, past the remains of his camp of the night before and off into the mountains, where I lost his tracks.

Thinking of lost...that Shannon was lost again. I sent him out to hunt, but he did not return. This time, though, he was only gone for four days. He had gone up the wrong branch of the river to follow us and had to backtrack. He had killed three deer and lived plentifully on his trip, but he looked a good deal worried by the time he finally found us.

On August 10 Captain Lewis set out again. This time he took McNeal and Shields to accompany him, and Drouillard, who had become Meri's favorite among all the men in our small band of brothers. And with good reason, for no man ever bettered George Drouillard on the trail. He left your father with me so that I could familiarize myself again with all his ailments and complaints.

Your mother had told us that we were close now to the summer camping grounds of her people, and her words, as usual, turned out to be true. Only the next day, Captain Lewis caught his first sight of an Indian. The man was on horseback and about two miles from him. Meri raised his glass to his eye. By the look of his dress, that Indian was from a different nation than we had yet seen. He had to be a Shoshone. It was a level plain and there was nothing to do but to walk toward the man in plain sight. When Captain Lewis was a mile away, the man stopped his horse. He had no weapon other than a bow and a quiver of arrows, and he'd surely seen Meri's gun by then. But the man sat his fine horse steadfast and waited.

Pulling his blanket from his pack, Captain Lewis made what he hoped would be recognized as a sign of friendship. He held the blanket by two corners and flapped it up into the air, bringing it down as if spreading a robe for a guest to be seated on. But the man did not take the invitation. He just sat and watched from the edge of the plain, close to the thick brush of a creekbed.

McNeal had come up behind Captain Lewis now. Meri handed him his gun and his pouch. Pulling out a handful of beads and a looking glass, he held those trinkets over his head and began to walk toward the Indian. When he was close enough to be heard, about two hundred paces away, Captain Lewis shouted out that word your mother had taught him.

"Ta-ba-bone," he hollered, "Ta-ba-bone!" The man narrowed his eyes and looked a bit confused as Meri pulled down his sleeve to show the whiteness of his skin.

But the other two members of the party had also begun to approach the Indian from different directions. Though

Captain Lewis signaled for them to stop, only Drouillard understood. Shields kept coming. And when Meri was a hundred paces from the mounted man, the Indian suddenly turned his horse around, gave him the whip, leaped up the creek, disappeared into the willow brush, and was gone.

The next day brought them no further Indians. But they did reach the place where the main branch of the Missouri, that great river we had traveled so many weary miles, narrowed at last to a rivulet. McNeal stood laughing with one foot on either side of that stream which had seemed so endless.

"Dear Lord, I do thank you," McNeal said, "for allowing me to live long enough to bestride the mighty Missouri!"

And over the next ridge Captain Lewis found another creek flowing to the west. Drinking its ice-cold waters, he deemed it the start of that stream which would take us to the Pacific, the great Columbia River. It was a day that brought a smile, however brief it might have been, to the face of my dear old friend.

There were no smiles on the faces of those of us still struggling to bring our boats up the Missouri. The men were complaining, and rightly so, of the immense labor they were obliged to undergo. There was one rocky shoal after another to drag the heavy canoes across. It was all I could do to persuade them that we should not leave the river and strike out overland. I had promised Captain Lewis I would rendezvous with him farther along, at the forks of a river we had named for President Jefferson. Fortunate it was that I kept to my word, or all that we had done might have come to naught.

Two days after their first sighting of the mounted Shoshone, Captain Lewis and Drouillard and McNeal once again encountered your mother's people. Looking up from a small valley, they saw two women, a man, and some dogs on the hill above them. Instead of fleeing, the three Indians watched them with some attention as they came closer.

"Halt," Meri said to his two companions. "Wait here." Then leaving off his rifle and pack, Meri broke out an American flag and strode toward the Indians.

"*Ta-ba-bone,*" he shouted as loudly as he could, waving the flag back and forth. "*Ta-ba-bone!*"

Turning away from him, first the two women and then the man vanished over the hill. When he reached the top, only the dogs remained, and they had little to say to him.

But Captain Lewis knew he was now on the right trail. He signaled the two men to join him, and they began to backtrack the Indians. It was an easy road to follow, dusty and much traveled by men and horses. The land was cut by steep ravines concealed from each other, and as they reached the head of one they suddenly came in sight of three Indian women, no more than thirty paces away. The young woman in the trio immediately fled into the brush and was lost from sight. The elderly woman and the young girl remained. They were much alarmed, but saw they could not escape.

Imagining the worst, the old woman and the little girl seated themselves on the ground and lowered their heads. Meri came up to them slowly. He took the old woman by her hand and gently raised her to her feet.

"*Ta-ba-bone,*" he said in a soft, reassuring voice. Then he stripped up his shirt sleeve and showed his white skin—for his hands and face, so long exposed to the sun, were as dark as any Indian's.

The little girl rose up to stand by the side of the old woman, their faces no longer fearful as Captain Lewis handed them beads, moccasin awls, and a little paint.

"George," he said to Drouillard, "ask her to call back that young woman who fled."

Using sign language, Drouillard did just that, and the old woman gladly obeyed. The fugitive soon returned, much out of breath but well pleased as Meri bestowed an equivalent portion of trinkets on her as well. Then, remembering what your mother had suggested, he took out the vermilion paint and painted the cheeks of all three of the Indian women as an emblem of peace.

Take us to your camp to meet your chiefs and warriors— Drouillard signed. Then they set off down the road. They went no more than two miles before they were met by a party of about sixty warriors mounted on excellent horses, coming at near full speed. Clearly the first Indians Meri had seen had raised the alarm. Again Meri put down his gun and advanced with the flag. The chief and two others rode up and listened to the words the old woman spoke as she showed them her gifts.

With that, the chief and the other two men leaped off their horses and advanced on Meri. One after another they embraced him, pressing their cheeks against his as they loudly said, *"Ah-hi-e, ah-hi-e."* Soon Meri was being smothered in one such hug after another by every man in that band of warriors, each one eager to let him know the white men were welcome and the Indians much rejoiced to meet them. By the time the Shoshones were done with their greetings, Captain Lewis and Drouillard and McNeal were besmeared with their grease and paint.

"Billy," Captain Lewis said to me later, "glad as I was to be so welcomed, I soon grew heartily tired of the national hug."

When all were seated in a circle, Captain Lewis took out the pipe of peace that he carried with him, filled it in the proper way with tobacco and offered it to them. As it was passed about the circle, each of the Shoshone men would take off his moccasins before smoking it. This was, we learned, their way of expressing the sincerity of their profession of friendship when accepting the pipe of a stranger. This gesture is to say, "May I go barefoot over the prairie if my words are false," a pretty heavy penalty if they are to march through the cactus plains of their country.

◈◆◈

The man who headed that party of Shoshones was their great chief. Cameahwait was his name. He led Meri and the others to their main camp, where they smoked the chief's pipe while sitting on green boughs and the skins of antelopes. The chief explained that they had feared Meri and his men to be scouts for a band of Pahkees, as they call the Minnetarees from Fort de Prairie. Just that spring those Pahkees had attacked them, and twenty of Cameahwait's people had been killed or taken prisoner. Many of their horses had been taken and all of their buffalo-skin lodges had been destroyed. All they had to live in now were the lodges that Captain Lewis saw around him, cones made of woven willow brush. Because of their enemies, they were unable to do much hunting. There were no buffalo here, only a few elk and deer. There were many antelope, but they were swift and difficult to kill. With only bows and arrows to use, they could not succeed most times when they hunted here in the mountains. They had little food to eat. And indeed everyone in the camp, from the smallest child to the oldest woman, looked thin and hungry.

All that we have—Cameahwait signed—*are berries to eat.*

Then he gave Meri and Drouillard and McNeal cakes made of serviceberries and chokecherries that had been dried in the sun.

What he told them of the land ahead of them was discouraging. The rivers that flowed toward the sunset—where he had been informed that white men like us lived near the great lake—were too rocky and swift to travel with canoes. The mountains were many and impossible to cross. Below the river junction there were no trees big enough to make canoes, only small cottonwoods and willows and berry bushes.

Their stay with the Shoshones was pleasant, though there was little to eat. They were much impressed with the fineness of the horse herd, which Drouillard estimated at four hundred animals, including several horses and mules with Spanish brands on them. They watched a group of twenty mounted men try to hunt a herd of ten antelope, but though they wore out their horses chasing them all morning, the antelope flew over the prairie like birds, and not a one was killed. Poor and hungry as they were, they shared whatever they had with Captain Lewis and his men, and the Indians danced and sang for the men's amusement till midnight.

The next day, though, things were not so good. Cameahwait and his warriors had promised to accompany Meri to meet us at the forks of Jefferson's River. But now the Indians were reluctant.

Foolish people among us say you are allies of the Pahkees— Cameahwait signed. *They think you lead us to be attacked and killed.*

"Tell the chief," Meri instructed Drouillard, "that we are sorry they do not trust us. Tell him they do not know white men and so we forgive them. Tell him that among white men it is disgraceful to lie or entrap an enemy by falsehood. Tell him that we hope there are some warriors among his people who are not afraid to die."

Yes, Pomp, I know. Even as a child you have lived among white men long enough to know that we do tell lies. But how else was Meri to convince the Shoshones to come with him? Without the Shoshones and their horses, we would surely have failed to reach our goal. And by suggesting that the warriors were afraid of death, he put them on their mettle. No man among them wanted to be thought a coward. Every one of those Indians declared he would go with Captain Lewis.

But now Meri had to find the rest of us. And that turned out to be not so easy a task as he had expected. When he arrived at the river where he expected us to be waiting, we were not there. Our progress up the Beaverhead had been so slow and painful that we were yet many miles away. The chief and all the other Indians in their party were now hanging back and looking ready to give up the quest. Then Meri remembered. He had written a note to me, asking me to bide in that place until he arrived back there. If we had not yet made it this far along the river, that note should still be there.

My brother chief may have found it difficult to reach this place so quickly with our canoes—he had Drouillard sign to Cameahwait. *He agreed to send a message ahead for me and leave it on one of our talking leaves.*

Then Captain Lewis had Drouillard and one of the chief's warriors go to that spot so the Indian could see him take the note from the forked stick. When Drouillard brought the note back, Meri made a great show of unfolding it and reading it. Even thought it was the same note Captain Lewis himself had written, he pretended it was from me and that it said I had been delayed by the difficulty of the water.

Yes, Pomp, it was a falsehood. He was deceiving those

trusting Indians. But it was all that Meri could think of, and he confessed to me that it did sit a little awkward with him to be so deceitful. So he spent another night camped out with them—many of the Shoshones avoiding the fire but sleeping hidden in the willow brush for fear that an ambush, indeed, was all that the future held in store for them. If we did not come into sight the next day, Captain Lewis knew, things would not go well.

21

SACAJAWEA

Reunion

Long ago, Gray Wolf and Coyote were out walking around. It was before anyone had died. But they knew that one day death would enter the world. They came to the Salmon River.

"How shall we decide about the way death will be?" Gray Wolf said.

"Let's do it this way," said Coyote. "You speak first about death, and I will speak last."

Gray Wolf picked up a piece of wood.

"I think it should be this way when people die," Gray Wolf said. "I will throw this wood into the water. If the wood floats, then people will die, but after four days have passed they will come back to life again."

Then Gray Wolf threw the piece of wood into the water and it floated. "Ah-hi-e!" Gray Wolf said. He was pleased. But Coyote had not yet spoken, and it was now Coyote's turn.

Coyote picked up a stone. "I think it should be this way," Coyote said. "I will throw this into the water. If it floats, then it will be as you said. But if it sinks, then people will die and not come back to this world again."

Then Coyote threw the stone into the water. It sank, and so, because Coyote spoke last, that was the way death came

into this world. People died and they did not come back to life.
    "This is how it should be," Coyote said. "If everyone just
kept on living, the world would be too crowded."

T HE CLOSER WE CAME to seeing my people, the more I
felt as Coyote's wife must have felt. Each time we came
close, they fled from us. Would I ever reach those with whom
I had once lived, those who knew me as a little girl? Would I
ever see my family and my friends? Or had they gone to a
world even more distant than the villages of the Minnetarees?
I dreamed at night about talking and laughing with my
people, but each morning when I woke, my dreams had still
not become real. I wondered if those dreams would ever come
true.

⋄⋅⋄

By now Captain Lewis had been gone many days. Our trip
up the river past the Beaverhead Hill had been a very hard
one. The men had suffered so much. Sometimes as they waded
in the cold water, the canoes would swing around in the current and knock them down, bruising them and almost drown-
ing them. Many of the men had wounds and great sores on
their bodies. Your good uncle was still unable to walk far because of how badly his feet had been hurt by so much walking
and by the thorns of the cactus.

Your good uncle was very worried about his brother captain. That morning he decided your father and I should walk
out with him. We would walk ahead of the boats to the place
where the rivers forked.

It was a good morning. The serviceberries were ripe and I picked them as I went along. Because his feet were so bad, Captain Clark could not go quickly, and so there was no hurry.

Suddenly I saw a little group of people coming down the valley ahead of me, through the high grass that still sparkled with the morning dew. Several Indians were coming toward us on horseback. I rubbed my eyes. Could it be true? They were wearing clothing that looked so familiar.

"Look," I said to Charbonneau, "look." I jumped up and down. Your father, catching my excitement, began to jump up and down with me. As Captain Clark came up to us, I spoke with my hands.

My people—I signed to him, pointing with my lips at them and then sucking my fingers. *They are my people!*

Soon they had reached us and jumped off their horses to embrace us. One of them was not a Shoshone at all. It was George Drouillard, wearing an ermine robe. My people must have given him that robe to honor him. It meant that he and Captain Lewis had been welcomed by them. It meant all would be well between our party and the Shoshones.

"I am Numi," I said to the Indian men.

"We are also the People," they said back to me in the men's language of our people. Their words were more beautiful to me than any song. I did not recognize among them any friends or family, yet I knew that I had finally come home. What I did not know was how much sadder and sweeter my reunion soon would become.

As we went along to reunite with Captain Lewis at their village, those young warriors could not resist asking me questions.

"When were you taken by the Minnetarees?" one of them

said. He was carrying Drouillard's gun. Drouillard had given it to him to carry, to prove that he was not leading them into an ambush.

"Is it true that you have a man among you who is as black as the charcoal from a fire?" said another.

They were so excited they could hardly wait for my answers. One of them held up a trade mirror given him by Captain Lewis.

"Do your friends have many things like this among them?" he said. "Look, it is like hard water! And it is brilliant like the sun sometimes. Other times it shows me my face."

"Five winters ago," I said. "...Yes, he is named York and is my friend...Wonderful things like that are as common among these people as pebbles along the shores of the river. They have great power."

That gave them much to think about. They rode for a while in silence.

"Maybe," said the first young man who had spoken, "it is true what your pale-skinned friends say. Maybe they will give us many guns like this one to keep. Then the Pahkees will no longer be able to raid us. We will be able to go out onto the plains and hunt buffalo whenever we wish. We will no longer have to hide in the mountains and starve."

I looked more closely at him and the other Shoshone men. In my excitement I had not noticed before how thin they all were, how the bones of their faces showed so clearly. I hoped that what he said would become true for my people.

22

WILLIAM CLARK

The Welcome

August 17th. Saturday. 1805.

Those people greatly pleased. our hunters killed three deer &
an antilope which was eaten in a Short time the Indians
being so harassed & compelled to move about in those rugid
mountains that they are half Starved liveing at this time on
berries & roots which they geather in the plains. Those people
are not begerly but generous, only one has asked me for
anything and he for powder.

JOURNAL OF WILLIAM CLARK
SHOSHONE COVE, IDAHO

WHAT A DAY that was for us all, Pomp! After we met
Drouillard and the few scouts sent ahead with him, we
proceeded to the place by the forks where Captain Lewis was
camped awaiting us. There were sixteen more Shoshone men
and women there with him. Their main chief had gone back
to the camp, Camp Fortunate we called it, to make ready our
welcome, so we did not meet him just then.

"Billy," Meri said to me as we shook hands amid the bliz-
zard of Shoshone hugs that came at me from all directions,
"these poor people are starved."

And it was the truth. Not a one of them—man, woman, or

child—had an extra ounce of flesh on his or her bones. Meri told me later how Drouillard managed to shoot a deer for them, and the starving men with him immediately cut open its belly to eat the guts raw. They behaved more like a parcel of famished dogs than like men. Yet he also noticed that they did not touch any of the better meat of the deer, but ate only those parts that they felt Meri and his companions would not want for themselves.

Hungry and savage as they were, they behaved better than most civilized gents would in such a state. When Captain Lewis took only one haunch of that deer for himself and gave the rest to the Shoshones, who had enjoyed no success at hunting for weeks, they were mightily gratified, thanking him again and again. I saw right away that we would have to do some serious hunting for these poor devils with no firearms.

But any discussions Meri and I might have had at that moment of reunion was brief. As soon as we were done with the round of national hugs, the whole party of Indians started to sing. They sang the whole way to Camp Fortunate.

◈◈◈

Ah, you are right, Pomp. I'm forgetting something. Where was your mother during this first welcome? As you might guess, she was beside herself with joy at meeting her very own people. She and your father had been the first to sight the oncoming Indian horsemen, whose party included Drouillard, who seemed a very Indian himself that day, all dressed in a fine Shoshone ermine mantle. When I limped up to them, your parents were dancing about together as if doing a jig, your mother shouting and waving and sucking her fingers to let me know those were her people.

Excited as she was then, it was to get even better for our

Janey. As soon as we reached the place where Captain Lewis was waiting, one of the women among those sixteen Indians recognized her. She ran up to your mother and about knocked her off her feet in an embrace. The two of them began talking and laughing all at once. They were both filled with excitement. It turned out she was a friend from your mother's childhood. Her name was Jumping Fish. The two of them had done everything together. That day when the Minnetarees took your mother and Otter Woman, they had captured Jumping Fish as well. But she had always been a great runner. Somewhere along the way she had managed to escape and make her way back home to her nation. She had been certain she would never see Sacajawea alive again.

◈

When we got to Camp Fortunate, the Indians had a kind of a shade made of willow branches woven together all prepared for us. The camp was set up in a circle, with antelope skins laid down on top of evergreen boughs for us to sit. The three chiefs met me with great cordiality and embraced me. They did it more restrainedly than had been the case with those first Shoshones we met. Being chiefs, they were supposed to control their emotions and keep their dignity. But you could see they were all as pleased as Punch about our visit.

The main chief—Cameahwait was his name—came up to me. Yes, I know who he is, Pomp. But when there's a surprise in a story you have to be patient and work up to it. Cameahwait was only one of his names. He also had a war name: Tooettecon'l. That meant Black Gun and it showed how important guns—or the lack of them—were to your mother's people. He owned one of the only two guns your people had back then, even though he didn't have any ammunition for it.

Cameahwait, his everyday name, meant something like Always on a Horse. As their main chief, he was the one who came up to me where I had been seated on a white skin. He tied to my hair six small pieces of shell that resembled pearls.

Meri caught my eye as he did that. He looked at that new jewelry of mine and mouthed the word, "Seashells!"

Captain Lewis was hoping that we were only a few days' journey from the ocean and that those shells were a sign of how close we were. In truth, those shells did come from the nations residing near the seacoast, and they were much valued by the Shoshones. But they obtained them from the Flatheads, who got them from the Nez Percé, who got them from the Wanapam, and so on, in a long chain of trade from one nation to the next, across the mountains and down the Columbia River.

◆◇◆

I had taken off my moccasins, as had Meri and the Indians. Cameahwait's green stone peace pipe made its way around our new circle of friends. That done, we were ready to have our first conference. Captain Lewis could hardly wait to have your mother start her work as interpreter. He had managed to say the basic things by means of sign, but there was a great deal he still needed to convey to the chief. Our great need for finding a way through the mountains and for horses were the two most important things to our group.

Up till now, our Janey had been busy with her old friend, the two of them sitting together off to the side. They were whispering when they thought they could not be heard.

"Charbonneau," I said, "ask our interpretess if she'd like to join us."

Then your father went over to your mother and brought

her into our little group. He was about to sit her down by the chief's side so she could hear his words and give ours back to him. But before he could reach her, she peered over at the chief for the first time. I could see her face and it appeared she had been hit by a bolt of lightning. And just about as swift as lightning, she leaped up and ran across the circle, right to Cameahwait, who looked as if he was recognizing her, too. As he stood up, she pulled off her blanket and threw it over both their heads—you know the way your people do when they want to share a moment of privacy, Pomp. Then as she embraced him, she cried profusely.

Charbonneau looked at us. He lifted up his palms.

"The chief," your father said, "he seems to be her family."

23

SACAJAWEA

New Names

One day Coyote's wife died. On that day he changed his mind about death. He decided it was better that people not stay dead forever. So he went to the place where the spirits of those who have died stay. It was a long journey. When he got there those who had died greeted him. His wife was glad to see him.

"I thought you would never come here," she said to her husband.

"I am only visiting," Coyote said.

Then he put his wife's spirit into a basket and started carrying her back to this world. If he could get all the way back without opening the basket, she would be able to come back to life. It went well for a few days, but it was a long journey. Coyote began to wonder how his wife's spirit was doing.

"It would not hurt to take a look and see if she is well," he said to himself. Then he opened the basket just a crack. But that was enough. As soon as he opened it, the basket was empty. Coyote's wife was gone. And ever since then no one has ever come back to this world after they have died.

DID CAPTAIN CLARK NOT MENTION how Stays Here acted when he saw you for the first time? Yes, he was very glad. It was as if I had come back from the land of the dead. Usually, when one of our people was taken captive by the Minnetarees, they would either escape soon or never be seen again.

But you must remember that as the chief it was his job first to think for the people. At that moment he had to speak for his nation. Their hunger was more important than his joy.

Even so, as I held you in my arms while I sat next to him, he would look over now and then at you. Then his eyes would meet mine briefly and a small smile would come to the side of his mouth. From the very first, you were important to your uncle Stays Here.

◆◇◆

It was not easy for me to translate. My eyes kept filling with tears. My voice caught in my throat. There was so much happiness for me that day. I had been reunited with my dearest friend from childhood, Jumping Fish, who had earned her new name when she tried to escape the Minnetarees by running across the river. It had not taken her long to start teasing me just as she used to do in the old days. She called me not Boat Pusher, but Wadze Wipe, Woman Who Was Lost. When I let her hold you, she got that familiar mischievous look in her eyes.

"Look," she called out. "My good sister Lost Woman has given me a son to adopt. He has been too much trouble for her. Now I will keep him."

But she gave you back to me. I would never have allowed anyone or anything to take you from me when you were a baby, Firstborn Son.

When I had grown calm enough, we began the business of translating. It was slow. First Captain Lewis would speak. I was understanding more of his words now. After all those many moons of travel with the white men, their language was no longer quite so strange to me. Then Labiche would speak those same words in French, another language I could understand in a small way, to your father. Charbonneau would try to repeat them to me in Minnetaree. Only then would I change all those languages into words that really made sense by speaking our beautiful language as only a Shoshone woman can.

As I translated the words of Captain Lewis, I also explained to your uncle Stays Here that the two captains were brave and honorable men. They had great power and their spirit helpers were very strong. Wherever they went, they tried to bring peace. They would help our people however they could. They would be followed by other men who would trade with the Numi. Those men would bring guns so that our people could hunt and defend themselves against the Pahkees. First, though, our party had to make its way to the Great Water That Tastes Bad on the other side of the mountains. To do that, the two captains needed to trade for horses. They had many useful things to trade, though they did not have enough guns with them to give any of their weapons to the Numi.

It was the season when your uncle should have been leading the people west to hunt buffalo. Everyone in the village deeper in the mountains was half starved. It was not an easy thing for him to decide to help the captains now.

But without help the white men would not succeed. They needed not just horses. They needed Indians to help them carry their baggage. They needed guides to lead them across the mountains.

"These men," I said, "have treated me like a daughter." I put my palm against your cheek as you slept in your cradleboard. "They have treated your nephew here like a grandchild. I am your only living sister, so I ask you as your relative. I ask you to help them."

It was true. Your uncle had whispered to me the sad news as we stood together with our heads close under my blanket. All of our family except for one other brother had been killed. The raids by the Pahkees and the Minnetarees, and the hard hungry winters, had taken our parents and all our other sisters and brothers. So the tears that I wept had been tears of joy and of sorrow. I was given much that day, but I also found out how much I had lost.

In the village Captain Lewis was able to trade for as many horses as our people could spare. He no longer seemed as worried as he had been. Some days later your good uncle Captain Clark joined us there. He had scouted the rivers and seen no way for us to continue along them. The only way to go would be to cross the mountains into the land of the pierced-nosed Indians on the other side.

There was an old man among our people who had traveled that way across the Lolo Pass with a group of the Nez Percé. It would be a very hard journey, Stays Here told them. But with the old man and his son to guide them, it would take our party only a few days. We did not know then just how long and hard a journey lay ahead.

24

WILLIAM CLARK

The Terrible Trail

September 3rd. Tuesday, 1805—

*hills high & rockey on each Side, in the after part of the day
the high mountains closed the Creek on each side and obliged
us to take on the Steep Sides of those Mountains. So Steep
that the horses could Scurcely keep from Slipping down,
Several sliped & injured themselves verry muvch, with great
dificuelty we made———miles & encamped on a branch of
the Creek we assended after crossing Several Steep points &
one mountain, but little to eate*

*The mountains to the East covered with Snow, we met
with a great misfortune, in haveing our last Thermometer
broken, by accident. This day we passed over emence hils and
Some of the worst roads that ever horses passed....*

JOURNAL OF WILLIAM CLARK
BITTERROOT MOUNTAINS

WHAT WAS OUR JOURNEY over those mountains like,
Pomp? Was there no other way we could have gone?
My scouting of the Salmon River showed me clearly that we
could not take boats down it. That was when Cameahwait in-
troduced me to Old Toby. He was a man who loved to wander
and had been more places than any other man in their tribe.

I asked him about the way to the southwest. The lands there were barren, he told me, hard desert. Not only that, the tribes there were hostile and we would be entering into the lands of the Spanish. Both he and Cameahwait said the road over the mountains, which rose above us higher than any mountains I had ever seen before, was our only way.

"No one," your uncle Cameahwait said, "can cross over those mountains so late in the season. The road is a very bad one."

But time was now running out for us. We had to reach the ocean before the winter. There was no thought of turning back. Old Toby saw things differently from your uncle. He had been that way before with the Nez Percé Indians. He would guide us, and his son would help him.

On September 1 we set out into the mountains. Old Toby led the way. The going was even harder than Cameahwait had described it. There were thickets through which we were obliged to cut a road. Up and down steep hills we went, with the greatest risk and difficulty. The horses were in perpetual danger of slipping to their certain destruction. There was no game to be had, and we ate the last of our salt pork. Snow fell, and then we broke our last thermometer. That was a blow Meri found hard to bear, since we had faithfully recorded the temperatures every day of our travel until then.

Three days later we came to a huge valley in the midst of the mountains. The Indians there were allies of the Shoshones and had a great camp in the Bitterroot Valley. Three Eagles, their chief, had been out scouting and saw us coming. He hid in the brush, thinking we might be enemies. When he saw York, all black as if painted up for war, that really worried him. But then he saw your mother and you. Raiding parties never took along a woman and a child. He also saw we didn't have blankets and we all looked worn and tired. Figuring we were not acting like a war party, he went back to the village and told his people to wait for us to arrive.

Once again we were subjected to the national hug and treated as welcome guests. They shared what food they had, which was little. They said they were Flatheads, making the sign of pressing their hands to either side of their head. Their name for themselves was Ootlashoots, the people of the Red Willow River. They were all about to ride out over that tough trail we'd just taken, to join the Shoshones on the buffalo hunt.

Their language was far different from Shoshone, and neither Old Toby nor your mother could speak it. But there was a Shoshone boy who'd been taken captive by a northern tribe and then freed by the Flatheads. He'd decided to stay with the Ootlashoots and spoke their language well. He was able to help translate.

Both our parties were in a hurry to take to the trail, but we spent a good two days there at a camp we dubbed Travelers' Rest. Mostly we were horse trading. The Indians were generous. They took some of the poorer horses we had in exchange for better ones. By the time we were done we'd added fourteen fine horses to our herd and were in good shape to continue on our way. The mountains ahead of us, one of the Ootlashoots said, were much harder than those easy ones we had just navigated.

I hoped they were just joking, in the way Indians will do with someone they like.

"How long will it take to cross those mountains?" I asked two of those Indians, who said they'd been on the Lolo Trail to visit the Nez Percé on the other side.

Perhaps they did not really know or were trying to encourage me.

"Only a handful of days," one of them said, holding up five fingers.

But it turned out to be three times that number, Pomp.

Sergeant Gass looked up at the peaks ahead of us as we left the Bitterroot Valley. "These are the most terrible mountains I ever beheld," he said.

And right from the start they were. The trail was well marked at first, and then it gradually seemed to vanish into thickets and downed timber. Snow was falling, and sleet. Even Old Toby became confused and led us off the track more than once. I was as wet and as cold as I had ever been in my life. Almost the only blankets we had were those in which you and your mother were wrapped. We'd traded everything else for the horses. To see the men wake up in the morning, shaking off the snow and struggling to wrap rags around their feet, was a painful sight.

Sergeant Gass came up to me that morning. "Captain," he said, "will we ever escape this horrible mountainous desert?"

"We will," I said.

Good man that he was, that was enough for him.

Two days later we saw that we'd soon have to start eating our pack animals. I pressed ahead with a party of hunters, leaving whatever food we could get cached for the main party and hoping to find the way out of those unforgiving mountains. We prayed for the trail to end. And on September 20 it did. We came out on a little upland plain. Smoke rose in the distance from the lodges of the Nez Percé.

25

SACAJAWEA

Quamash

Quamash *is a round root, about the size of your fist. But at the start of the world, when Wolf was placing all the good roots into the ground for the Numi to dig, he did not put* quamash *in our land. Maybe it was Coyote who placed that root in the ground, for it is tricky and very strong. If you have not eaten it from childhood, it will not recognize you. It will start to dance and complain inside your stomach.*

"I do not belong here," Quamash will sing.

Yes, Firstborn Son, that journey over the great mountains that rose up like wolves' teeth was a terrible one. Your good uncle has described it to you well. All through that trip there were no complaints. Even your father did not complain, though perhaps he was only too cold and tired to do so. But did Captain Clark tell you what happened to him and Captain Lewis when we reached the Nez Percé? Did he tell you about the *quamash* bread? I am not surprised that he forgot to tell you this, for it was not his favorite food. He and all of his men, they became sick after *quamash* bread. They were so weak from it that they could barely stand up.

When Captain Lewis came out of the mountains two days later, Captain Clark warned him not to eat the *quamash* bread. But Captain Lewis did not listen. He was so hungry that he ate twice as much as Captain Clark had eaten. All the other men joined in the feast. When they began to be sick, Captain Lewis decided to use the big medicine. It was a large pill that everyone took when they were ill. It was so strong that it could cure almost anything. But *quamash* did not like the big medicine.

"Big medicine," the *quamash* said, "I will fight you and you will lose."

Then everyone who took Captain Lewis's pills became even sicker than before. Captain Lewis was the sickest of all. They were as weak as little babies for many days. Even while Captain Clark, who had learned to respect *quamash*, was off with our friend York and some other men who had not eaten so much, making new canoes from the big pine trees, Captain Lewis was still unable to walk around. For some reason, though it made your father very sick, *quamash* liked me. Maybe that was because I was not from as far away as the others in our party. It did not make you or me sick. So I was able to help take care of the men when they were not well.

◆◇◆

This is an important story, my son. Because it shows you what kind of good people those Nez Percé were. They were at war with their enemies to the north and the west. They had few weapons. Just like our Numi, they needed guns. While all the men in our party were sick, they could have taken those guns from us. They could have killed all of our men with no trouble at all. But no one lifted a hand to steal anything or to harm any of our party. Instead they treated us as if we were relatives returned from a long absence. They proved that the Nez Percé are an honorable nation who know how to treat their guests.

Maybe it was because of Watkuweis. She said her name to me in her strange language and then made signs to show it meant Woman Who Went Far Away and Came Back. She was a Nez Percé woman who had been taken captive by our enemies the Pahkees. They took her far to the north, where a white trader bought her freedom. She stayed with him for several winters before making her way back to her people. She smiled at all the sick white men and then signed to me—*Those people treated me well. I will tell my people to do them no harm.*

Our stay with the Nez Percé was not a long one. We were there long enough for all the men to recover and for Captain Clark to make canoes near the river whose waters ran deep and clear toward the sunset. The Nez Percé helped with the canoe making. They showed your good uncle how to make a canoe faster by putting it over a fire to burn out the center.

Twisted Hair, the chief of the village, liked the captains. He drew a map of the country to the west on a piece of white elkskin. Then he and another chief said they would go with us at least part of the way.

"We will walk ahead of your canoes and tell our people that you are friends," Twisted Hair said.

When I looked at the rushing waters of the Clearwater River, I thought that walking ahead was a good idea. It seemed as if no boats would be able to go down those rapids. But the captains and the men were not worried. After so many days of pushing and pulling against the current, they were excited at going downstream at last. Nothing could stop them now.

Old Toby and his son came to me as I stood on the shore with you in your cradleboard. Captain Lewis was about to start down the first of the bad rapids with two canoes.

"I think they are going to drown," Old Toby said.

"No," I said, "even though I will walk along the shore, that is not what I think."

Old Toby just shook his head. I knew he was saying good-bye in the way our people sometimes do. He was saying it not with words of farewell but by making it clear in other ways that he would soon be leaving.

The canoes made it through those rapids and through more such places where the river narrowed its throat and growled like a hungry animal. That night, when we had made camp and were all gathered about the fire, Old Toby and his son slipped away. They were seen running to the east along the riverbank.

The captains were sorry about this. They had not yet given Old Toby anything for the great help he gave them.

Twisted Hair—they signed—*can you send a horseman to bring them back so that we can say good-bye and pay them?*

Twisted Hair disagreed. *It is not a good thought*—he answered—*whatever you give them, the Nez Percé will take it from them.*

So no one was sent after them. When they reached Twisted Hair's village, Old Toby and his son were allowed to each take a horse from those we had left behind. Then they set out on the trail over the mountains, back to our people. If they hurried, they would be able to take part in the buffalo hunt.

141

26

WILLIAM CLARK

Many Rapids, Many Nations

October 14th, Monday. 1805——

passed rapids at 6 and 9 miles, at 12 miles we came too at the head of a rapid which the Indians told me was verry bad, we viewed the rapid found it bad in descending three Stern canoes stuck fast for some time on the head of the rapid and one struck a rock in the worst part, fortunately all landed Safe below the rapid which was nearly 3 miles in length....

In this Island we found some Split timber the parts of a house which the Indians had verry securely covered with Stone, we also observed a place where the Indians had buried their fish, we have made it a point at all times not to tak any thing belonging to the Indians even their wood. but at this time we are Compelled to violate that rule and take a part of the split timber we find here buried for firewood, as no other is to be found in any direction.

JOURNAL OF WILLIAM CLARK
SNAKE RIVER RAPIDS, WASHINGTON

It took us a full month, but that journey down the rivers to the Pacific Ocean seemed far swifter as I remember it. Just as there was one rapid after another, so were there many different nations along the rivers. Each nation would quickly give way to the next. For the first two weeks, our Nez Percé guides served us well. They went ahead to announce our arrival to the nations that were kin to them. So we were greeted with great warmth by the Yakimas, the Wanapams, and the Wallawallas.

As always, you and your mother were a great aid to us. All of the Indians were reconciled to our friendly intentions whenever they caught sight of the two of you. A woman with a party of men is a token of peace.

I remember one occasion in particular when your mother's presence proved that we were harmless. October 19 it was, the same day that I first saw the snow-tipped peak of one of the mountains that are laid down by Vancouver. We were then on the mighty Columbia. We came to an island where the people hid from us in fright. Pushing open the door of one lodge, a door made of woven reeds, I found thirty-two people sitting on the floor in great fear. They were crying, weeping, even banging their heads. I drew two of them outside and tried to get them to smoke with me.

It was not until the canoe came up with you and your mother that things changed. Then everyone who had remained within in great despair came outside and seemed to assume new life. Those Umatilla Indians explained that they had seen me shoot a crane just before we reached their island and it had filled them with fear. They had thought we were from the clouds and were not men. But the sight of an Indian woman with a baby had assured them of our humanity and our friendly intentions.

Because we were so well received, we were able to trade for food with the villages along the river, though the food was not especially to my liking. Most of the men learned to enjoy eating dog. Even Captain Lewis, whose great dog, Seaman, remained faithfully by his side, would eat the meat of the dogs that men and women would sell us. But I could never reconcile myself to that, and I grew heartily sick of smoked salmon.

There was almost no game to hunt along the rivers. Even fresh fish were not to be had. It was past the time of year when the salmon can be caught as they swim up the stream. There were still great numbers of dying and dead fish in the rivers. But their flesh was spoiled and we did not think it proper to use them.

❖

Whenever we came to a new rapid, there would be great crowds of Indians waiting for us. They were not there to assist us. They were there to watch, for we were going through stretches of rough and turbulent water into which no Indian would place a canoe. They were curious to see if we would survive, and we would hear great shouts of excitement and even singing from our onlookers onshore as we entered each narrow and dangerous stretch.

As always, we treated the people with great courtesy, showing respect to them and trading fairly for the things we needed. At first the nations along the upper part of the river showed hospitality and generosity. But that would change as we came closer to the ocean, just as we saw the houses and the ways of the people change. Soon after leaving the lands of the Nez Percé, the skin lodges gave way to oblong buildings covered with rush mats. Each village had its own graveyard marked by picket fences, quite unlike the burial scaffolds of the mountains and plains Indians.

I continually called Captain Lewis's attention to this changing scene, urging him to write down the details of all the new things we were seeing. But he was entering one of those times when writing no longer seemed possible for him. I thought then that it was nothing more than the necessity to keep his focus on the details of our journey. There was much to worry about, for our canoes were always in danger of tipping and losing our precious cargo of information that could never be replaced. He always had to be alert for danger.

Until we reached the first of the falls on the Columbia, there had been little to give us reason to fear the Indians. We had, however, noticed that thievery was becoming common. If we put anything down it would quickly disappear when our backs were turned. This was a surprise to us. We had grown accustomed to the honesty of such people as the Shoshones and the Nez Percé. On one occasion a young man of your mother's nation had walked many miles to return to Captain Lewis a knife that had been dropped by Drouillard when he rose after a night's rest.

Perhaps the people of the river felt that we were so wealthy we could easily part with some of the many things we owned. Or perhaps they were simply making us pay a toll for passage along their river. Whatever the reason, it soon reached the point where at all times and all places, we were on our guard.

Then Chief Twisted Hair, who had guided us so well, informed us that great danger did indeed lie ahead. The people of the nation below the great Celilo Falls were Chinooks, unfriendly to his people. The Nez Percé had recently been at war with them. His relatives among the local nations had learned that the Chinooks intended to kill us. Twisted Hair and his fellow chief urged us to turn back. They were ready to return home. They could be of no further help. They did not speak the language of the Chinooks and could no longer act as translators. With that in mind, Meri and I made certain that all of the rifles were in good condition and each man always had a hundred rounds of ammunition.

With all these concerns, I did not take much note of Captain Lewis's increasing silence. He could write in his journals later, I thought. I did not know there was something deeper hidden beneath the surface of those moods. It was, I think, an inner despair, a shadow of the sad fate that would befall my dear lost friend.

◆◈◆

Why was writing so important to us? Why did Captain Lewis write so much? Ah, think of it this way. You know how your mother tells you stories? Of course you do. Those stories delight you and also help you to remember, don't they? Well, that is what Meri was doing with his writing. Each time he saw something new, heard a word in another Indian tongue, viewed a new creature, or measured our position by the stars, he was hearing a new story. And by writing it down he ensured that those tales could be told to others.

27

SACAJAWEA

The Great Hungry Water

Long ago, there was a boy who did not respect the salmon people. When he was given a piece of salmon to eat, he threw it on the ground and stepped on it. But as he walked by the river, he slipped and fell into the deep water and drowned. His body was swept out to sea and he joined the salmon people. A year passed and he learned many things. At last the time came for the salmon to return to the river. Salmon Boy swam with them. As he swam past his old village, a woman caught him. She saw the salmon was wearing a copper bracelet on its fin. She knew it was her son. She took him to the medicine man. The medicine man worked and prayed for many days. Gradually Salmon Boy turned back into a human being. As a human, he taught the people many things they needed to know. The most important thing was that they always had to show thanks and respect to the Salmon nation.

Yes, it was as your good uncle said. Those Indians along the river were far different from our people in many ways. The smell of dead and dried fish permeated everything. Our people have long lived by our own river and we, too, are people of the salmon. But here there were fish skins everywhere upon the banks of the river. And the dried grass was full of fleas that swarmed upon us whenever we left our canoes.

Though they sometimes took blankets or knives from our camp, those nations along the river never threatened us with harm. Even after the two chiefs of the pierced-nosed people turned back, we were still welcomed at each village. In the evenings Cruzatte would play his fiddle and York would dance to amuse the Chinook people.

Things kept changing as we went down the river, which grew wider and swifter in its flow. The lodges were no longer made of grass mats. Now they were like these houses here in St. Louis, made of boards cut from big trees. Then fog and rain began. Every day was the same. We woke to see a world around as gray as smoke. It seemed as if we were traveling not upon the river but within it. The people along the river were used to that weather; they wore tall hats shaped like cones that shed the rain. But all that we could do, Firstborn Son, was get wetter and wetter.

The people there along the lower part of the river looked very different from any Indians I had seen before. As I have told you, few Indians are as good-looking as our own Numi. But these Indians did strange things to themselves. They had pierced holes in their noses and placed white pieces of shell, as long as one of your fingers, in them. Their heads were flattened and pointed on top. It was not the way they were born. They would take pieces of wood and fasten them on the heads of their babies to shape their heads that way. No, I do not think it hurt, but I would never allow that to be done to you, my son.

The boats of those Chinooks were very beautiful. They

were finely made, as graceful as the wings of birds. Those Chinook canoes were very light and strong and much easier to paddle than our boats. The fronts of their largest canoes lifted out of the water, tall as a man's height, and were carved into such shapes as men or bears. The captains would have liked to trade all our boats for such canoes, but they were not able to do so.

The further downriver we went into that gray land of fog and rain, the harder it became to bargain for things. The food was good to eat, especially *wapato* roots, which Captain Lewis liked very much. *Wapato* was kind to everyone's stomach and not quarrelsome like *quamash*. But those people asked such high prices, saying that the white men below would give great prices for anything. By now your good uncle and Captain Lewis had used up almost all of the trade goods. They had little left to trade with. Captain Lewis was looking more worried, even though we were getting close to seeing the Great Water That Tastes Bad.

◈◈◈

When we came to that water that tasted like salt, your good uncle was so happy he seemed ready to weep. Everyone was excited, even though it was still raining and there was no place where we could camp safely. Their hopes gave way to disappointment. There was no sign of any white traders on the coast. It seemed that the other white men they had hoped to find did not come there at that time of year. They had sailed away in their boats as big as houses. So there would be no way to send messages back to their homes and their great chief, Jefferson. We could not sail back home in one of those big boats. To get back home we would have to return the way we had come.

That first place where we reached the Great Water turned out to be a bad one. The shore was narrow and covered with stones. The water acted strangely there, my son. Even though there was no height of land for it to fall from, that wide water was like a waterfall. It lifted and rose and then came rushing toward us as if it wanted to swallow us up. Each day the water would fall back, as if it was gathering strength. Then it would come rushing in again, growing higher and higher. I did not see how anyone could have the courage to live so close to water that was so big and so eager to eat people.

For many nights we were caught there, between that hungry wide water and the rocky cliffs. We could not cross over to the other side of the river with our boats, for the wind and water drove us back each time. Thunder rolled over us and lightning struck the water. Huge trees came washing in. Some of those trees were big enough to crush a whole village. We had been wet for so long that our clothing was rotting. It had been a very long time since we had been able to make a fire.

❖

Finally, one afternoon, the wind stopped and the river became calm. Though it kept on raining, we were able to escape that small rocky place where we had almost been chewed up and eaten by the hungry water. We found an old empty village farther up the coast, on a sand beach near a small river. No one was living there and we were able to set up camp. People came to talk and trade. One day two Chinook chiefs came and had with them a beautiful robe made of the skin of sea otters. Captain Lewis wanted that robe very badly. But the chief who

150

owned it did not like anything he offered for trade. He offered a watch, red beads, handkerchiefs.

"No," said the chief. Then he pointed at my belt of blue beads. That was what he wanted in exchange for his robe.

Captain Lewis looked at me, hoping that I would agree.

Perhaps, I thought, *this will bring the sunshine into his heart again.*

As I took off my beautiful belt, Captain Clark removed his own coat of blue cloth and handed it to me. So it was that I lost my belt of beads and Captain Lewis was able to get that robe of sea otter skins.

Soon another group of Indians came to trade, bringing more sea otter robes. We no longer had any blue beads and so could not trade with them, for that was all they wanted. But these Indians were not Chinooks. They belonged, they told us, to the Clatsop nation, and they seemed friendlier than the Chinooks had been. They had once been a large nation, but now the Clatsops were few. Most of their people had died from a sickness of smallpox that came to them from the white traders.

The two captains had little liking for the Chinooks, especially Captain Lewis. So many things had been stolen from them by Chinook people that Captain Lewis thought them a nation of thieves. The Chinooks would not do anything for them unless they were paid. But the Clatsops seemed ready to help.

"There is a better place for you to camp," the Clatsops told the captains. "It is on the other side of the river. There are many elk there for you to hunt."

Now there was a decision to be made. Should we cross to the other side and make a winter camp there, or go back up the river? Captain Lewis was certain about what he wished to do. If we crossed to the other side it would be easier for us to get close to the big water, because it was not so rocky there. Then he could make salt. The winter would be harder upriver, and we could not cross the mountains until the snow melted. However, because it was such a big decision, the captains decided that everyone should take part.

"We will take a vote," your good uncle said. Then he made markings on his talking leaves that stood for each of the people in our party. Each person was asked what they wanted us to do. Should we go back up the river and make our winter camp by the falls? Should we stay in this place or cross to the other side?

Everyone was asked about the choice. Then Captain Clark would repeat their words and make marks on the talking leaves. Your father, Charbonneau, simply waved his hand when it was his turn.

"Charbonneau chooses to do whatever everyone else decides," Captain Clark said, making straight lines across the white leaf.

York, though, was very clear when his time to vote came.

"Cross over and examine," York said. "Then if it is not good, we can look upriver toward the falls."

Of all the men who voted, only John Shields wanted to go back up the falls without crossing to the other side. He had almost been crushed by a great log that washed into his canoe. He wanted to look at the wide hungry water no longer.

When it came to me, I made it clear how I felt.

"I choose to go wherever there are plenty of roots to dig," I said.

"Janey is in favor of a place where there's plenty of potatoes," said your good uncle.

So we decided to make our winter camp.

28

WILLIAM CLARK

At Fort Clatsop

Friday the 3rd. January 1806

At 11 A.M. we were visited by our near neighbour Chief or tia Co Mo wool alias Conia and six Clatsops. they brought for Sale Some roots berries and 3 Dogs also a small quantity to fresh blubber. this blubber they informed us they had obtained from their neighbours the Cal La mox who inhabit the coast to the S.E. near one of their Villages a Whale had recently perished. this blubber the Indians eat and esteem it excellent food. our party from necescity have been obliged to Subsist some length of time on dogs have now become extreamly fond of their flesh; it is worthy of remark that while we lived principally on the flesh of this animal we wer much more healthy and more fleshey than we have been Sence we left the Buffalow Country. as for my own part I have not become reconsiled to the taste of this animal as yet.

JOURNAL OF WILLIAM CLARK
FORT CLATSOP, OREGON COAST

YES, POMP, IT WAS JUST as your mother said. We crossed over the river and scouted that place recommended to us by the Clatsops. That coast was a terrible place. The rain and ocean swells brought great trees, some of them two hundred feet long, that threatened to crush us like grain in a mill. Many of our men were sick or hurt by the time we abandoned what we had called Cape Disappointment. Sergeant Pryor was unwell with a dislocation of his shoulder, Gibson with the dysentery, Fields with boils on his leg, and Werner with a strained knee. Even your old friend York was suffering with colic. And we were still beset with fleas, which bit every part of our bodies and gave us no rest at night. Nor would we ever be rid of those swarms of tormenting insects through that whole winter. On that coast, the fleas are so numerous and hard to get rid of that the Indians have different houses which they resort to occasionally.

Though the hunting had been good at first, there was not enough game to sustain us. *Wapato* root, dog meat, fresh and dried fish, cakes of salal berries—all had to come from the local Indians. Though we had little to offer, we needed to trade with the natives to survive that endless, cold, and wet winter. Our own clothing was ill suited to their land. We needed the woven native caps and capes when we dared venture out into the storms—though the weather seemed to bother the Chinooks and Clatsops not at all. As we huddled around our smoky fires while the rain streamed from the skies, they were out in their boats as if it were a sunny and calm day.

By the time it was early January, all of our trade goods were reduced to a mere handful that could be held in two handkerchiefs. With that small store of fishhooks, worn files, brass wire, moccasin awls, and beads, we managed to obtain enough to survive, but not with great comfort. However, the turn of the year brought new life to Captain Lewis. It was 1806 at last. In but two months we would be headed homeward. He began to write with more frequency in his journal, describing the people and their customs, the clothing of the women—which he heartily disapproved of—the carving of their great boats. Though one day was much like another, at least each new day brought us closer to departure.

The great fish? Ah, Pomp, your mother mentioned that to you. But you want me to tell you about it again, eh?

Part of the trade on that coast was in whale blubber and whale oil. The hats we wore showed men in boats going out to sea to strike those great fish, the whales, with their spears. How large were the whales? As large as this house in which we are now standing. In the Bible, you shall read more of how the good Lord sent one such creature to swallow up Jonah, long ago.

Word came to us that a whale had been washed up on-shore down the coast from our salt-making camp. I decided to go and see that leviathan in the hopes of getting a parcel of the blubber. When she heard of my plan, your mother insisted that she and your father be taken along. She observed that she had traveled a long way to see the great waters, and now that this monstrous fish was also to be seen it would be hard if she were not permitted.

When we reached that place it was a sight to behold. The great dark creature lay up on the beach, its tail still awash in the waves. A party of native women were busily engaged in cutting it up, taking off great sections as if cutting thick bark from a tree. Your mother carried you close so that you could reach out your small hands to touch its smooth sides and look deeply into one of its great open eyes. Ah, you think you remember that now? Perhaps you do, Pomp.

At last, though—at long last—that endless season ended. Since the seventh of December we had wintered and remained at that place and lived as well as we had any right to expect, notwithstanding the repeated fall of rain. We can say we were never one day without three meals of some sort, either poor elk or roots. The snows in the mountain passes would be gone or melting by the time we reached them. On March 23, we were packed and ready to depart. We gave over possession of Fort Clatsop and all the furniture we'd made to Chief Comowool. Off we went through Meriwether's Bay and around Meriwether's Point, up into the Columbia. We were on our way home.

29

SACAJAWEA

◇◆◇◆◇◆◇◆◇◆◇◆◇

Thieves

Long ago, strange people came to our land to hunt and fish. They were greedy and drove our people from their hunting grounds. They were great hunters with their bows and arrows and began to kill all of the game.

One of our medicine men went into the forest to pray for help from the spirits. He came to a place where wolves and mountain lions, bobcats and foxes were gathered. The chief of those animal spirits was a mountain lion with the head and hands of a human being.

"We will help you," said the Mountain Lion Chief, "if you promise never to kill or eat any fox or wolf or bobcat or mountain lion. In the future, never go to war without consulting us."

The medicine man promised. He returned to his people and told them what had happened. He said that the spirits had told them to go to the mountain. The people did as he said. Then a light appeared on the horizon. When the people reached the mountaintop they saw that it was the fire of lava flowing into the valley. The lava killed all of their enemies.

Since then our people have never hunted or eaten the wolf, the bobcat, the fox, or the mountain lion.

I SAW A HARD JOURNEY ahead of us as we set out from our winter camp. We had been wealthy when we left the Mandans, but now we were poor people, Firstborn Son. Almost all of our trade goods were gone, our clothing was worn-out, we had not much left to buy food. Worst of all, we soon heard that there was little or no food to be found upriver by the big waterfalls. Many canoes came past us. All of them carried hungry people from upriver who had used up all their winter food. The salmon would not come for another moon. One small group that stopped and talked with us were so hungry that they picked up the bones and little pieces of refuse meat we had left behind.

We passed one large village where we had not stopped on our trip down the river. The Chinook man who was guiding us up the river told the captains that all the people there, except for a few, had died of smallpox brought by the white men. Those Indians had gotten many bad things from the white traders. It seemed, here along the river and by the Great Water, as if knowing the white men had either killed the Indians or turned them into thieves. I hoped it would never be that way for our Numi. Firstborn Son, even though the white men bring many things that our people want, never allow anything to turn you into a person of no honor.

At last we came to the place where the big river became narrow, below the falls. The river in the narrows was too high and too swift for us to travel any farther by water. From then on we had to go by land to the villages of the Nez Percé, who had been asked to care for our horse herd over the winter. The two captains were able to buy some horses there near the falls. But the horses were not very good and the price for them was high. The captains had to use two of the big metal kettles that we cooked in to pay for them. As I said, Firstborn Son, we were very poor by then.

Captain Lewis was still angry at those river Indians who kept trying to steal from us and showed so little respect. We could go no farther in our canoes, but he did not want to let those bad people have them. He had a great fire made by the banks of the river. Then he ordered that all the canoes, the paddles, the poles, and everything else we were not taking with us should be put onto that fire and burned. Even while this was being done, one Indian sneaked in and tried to steal a piece of iron that had been taken from a paddle. Captain Lewis grabbed the man and hit him several times before having him thrown out of the camp. Then he made a speech to the Indians who had gathered around. Drouillard spoke to them in sign language as Captain Lewis shouted his words. Captain Lewis was now very, very angry.

"We will shoot anyone who tries to steal from us," he said. "We are not afraid to fight. We have the power to kill all of you and destroy your houses, but we do not wish to harm you if you do not take our things. Two of our tomahawks were stolen here today. We could take horses from you in return. But we do not know which men took the tomahawks, so we would rather lose our property than take from an innocent person."

Captain Lewis's words were very strong. The chiefs of the nearby village were there, and they hung their heads in shame when he had finished speaking. Nothing more was stolen from us after that.

With the few horses we had gotten, we set out toward the mountains. As soon as we left the river behind, the people acted differently. After a few more sleeps, we were among the

Wallawallas, who are relatives of the Nez Percé. They had met us the previous autumn, and their chief, Yellept, was very happy to see us again. He brought us to his village and gave everyone food.

There was a woman of our own Numi nation among them. She had been taken captive many years ago and she was happy to meet someone she could talk with in our beautiful language. Her name was White Crane. She was very kind to me and told me what a fine, strong child you were. Of course that was true. She also praised me too much for my courage in traveling so far.

"You are brave," she said. "Your name should not be Bird Woman, it should be Woman Chief."

With her help and mine as translators, the two captains were able to talk with Chief Yellept and learn much about the trail we must follow to find the Nez Percé. Once again, Captain Lewis smiled that small smile at me, and Captain Clark spoke words of appreciation that pleased me as much as if they had been said by my own father.

"You have done well, Janey."

That night the Wallawallas danced and sang in our honor. Some of the men in our party joined in the dancing, and that made the heart of the Wallawallas glad. We got good horses from them. Captain Clark traded his sword and Captain Lewis traded the beautiful pistol that he kept in a box. But the captains did not mind dealing with these honest people.

I will tell you how different the Wallawallas were from the river Indians who tried to steal everything from us. Two days after we left their village, three Wallawalla boys rode into our camp. They had been riding hard to catch up with us because they wanted to return a steel trap that one of the men in our party had left behind by accident.

Captain Lewis's eyes were moist as he thanked them.

I honor you for your honesty—he signed to the boys. *You are a nation of good hearts.*

30

WILLIAM CLARK

Doctoring the Nez Percé

Friday 23rd. May 1806

The child is something better this morning we apply a fresh poltice of the wild Onion which we repeeted twice in the course of the day. the swelling does not appear to increas any since yesterday. The 4 Indians who visited us to day informed us that they came from their village on Lewis's river two days ride from this place for the purpose of seeing us and getting a littl eye water. I washed their eyes with some eye water and they all left us at 2 P.M. and returned to the villages on the opposit side of this river.

JOURNAL OF WILLIAM CLARK
CAMP CHOPPUNISH, IDAHO

YOU SAY THAT YOU WANT to hear the story of how I saved your life when you were sick, Pomp? No, I am not a great doctor, no matter what your mother has said. All right, I shall tell you. But I will do so in my own way.

It happened soon after we left the Wallawallas. Good fortune was with us, for we came across a small band of the very people we were seeking, the Nez Percé. Not only that, there was an old friend of ours among them. It was their chief, Tetoharsky. He was the one who had accompanied Twisted

Hair that previous autumn and helped guide us to the river. He was overjoyed to see us, for many of his people had doubted our survival. Those good people had truly taken a liking to us during our brief stay.

Tetoharsky also remembered something I had quite forgotten. While we were staying with them, they had brought to us an old man who had been unable to walk for some time. I took some liniment and rubbed it on the old man's leg and thigh. I did it with some ceremony, knowing how important it is among the Indians to do things in a memorable way. Quite often, Pomp, when someone is ill it is because they are sick in their thoughts. A good doctor can often seem to produce miracles just by cheering someone up. My ministrations proved to be of use, it seems. The old man began to walk soon after that, and pronounced himself completely cured by my medicine. Now, though it was far from the truth, the Nez Percé thought I was a great healer!

I soon found myself nearly overwhelmed with patients. They seemed especially fond of me as a doctor, even though Captain Lewis knew far more of medicine than I. One of their most common complaints was sore eyes, brought about, I believe, by the smoke in their lodges and the poor diet of roots and dried fish they suffered through during the winter. On the morning of May 12, according to my journal, I treated no fewer than forty applicants with sore eyes. The eyewash I gave them was almost always effective, and such complaints as rheumatic disorders and soreness in their backs responded just as well to massages and poultices. I even managed, through the use of sweat baths, to ease the pain in the back of one of our men who had become unable to walk. My same use of sweat baths, along with a few drops of laudanum, even appeared to effect a cure on an old man who had been paralyzed and unable to move his limbs for some months. Poor as my medical skills were, I must admit that the Indians did seem to gain some benefit from them.

It was a fortunate thing that my doctoring was in such demand, for we had almost nothing left that we could use to trade for food and horses. The food was mostly *quamash* roots, which we had now grown used to and could digest as well as the Nez Percé, and such meat as the Nez Percé themselves would not eat. Yes, Pomp, we were still eating dogs and horses. The spring run of salmon had not yet reached their rivers, and the buffalo herds were on the other side of the Bitterroot Mountains, which were still closed off by snows more than ten feet deep.

◆◆◆

Things did not all go smoothly. When we finally met with Twisted Hair, he told us that he had not taken care of our horse herd, as he had promised to do. We had told Twisted Hair we would reward him with a gun when we returned. But Cut Nose, another of the chiefs, had quarreled with Twisted Hair soon after our departure, saying that he, Cut Nose, should have been the one to care for the horses. As a result, our horse herd had become scattered. We called both of the old men together and let each of them speak.

"Cut Nose spoke badly of the way I cared for your horses. I grew so tired of hearing his bad words that I stopped caring for the horses," said Twisted Hair.

"Twisted Hair is a bad old man with two faces," Cut Nose said.

We listened closely to both of the chiefs. After they had spoken, they no longer seemed angry at each other. Then, together, they helped us round up most of our horses, which were not in bad shape, and many of the saddles we had left behind. Then we gave Twisted Hair an old British musket that we had bought from a Chinook trader for two elk skins, and we promised another gun to Cut Nose when the rest of our horses and gear were brought in.

❖

It was soon after this that you became ill, Pomp. You were cutting your teeth and a fever came upon you. Your throat and neck swelled, and Captain Lewis and I were much worried. But your mother had such confidence in me that she did not fret or weep. Instead she placed you in my arms.

"You will cure him," she said.

Pomp, that may have been the most frightening time of that whole trip for me. I feared that my poor ability as a doctor would not help you. I gave you a dose of cream of tartar and flower of sulfur. I applied poultices of boiled onions. I held you in my arms and prayed for your health. Finally, after a few days, your health began to return. I cannot say for a certainty that it was my medicine that cured you. Ah, but your mother has assured you that it was, eh?

❖

Though I had no shortage of patients during the month we spent with the Nez Percé, my work as a healer did not bring in enough to provide us with all that we needed. We had expected to stay only a few days, but the snows of the previous winter had been heavier than usual. The Lolo Pass was not open, and we had to wait and wait, and wait even more. By now we were cutting the buttons from our coats to trade for food, and we had traded every blanket we could spare, so each of us had no more than a single blanket.

Our horse herd, though, had been greatly increased through our trade, and we had more than sixty fine animals. Of all the nations of the west, the Nez Percé surely have the largest and finest herds of horses, and as riders no one can compare with them. What a sight it was to see the way they rode down those steep hills at full speed! During that long time we had to wait, we grew even more close in friendship with those fine, honorable people. We engaged in every manner of game with them, and hard it was to beat them at anything.

It was only in shooting that they could not match us. Captain Lewis struck a mark 220 yards away with his rifle, causing them to much admire both his shooting—and his weapon. Like your mother's Shoshone people, the Nez Percé had been much troubled by the Blackfeet, who obtained guns from the British. Though no one could match the Nez Percé in the shooting of a bow from horseback, a man with a gun could easily defeat one who had only a bow. The great hope of the Nez Percé was that we would send many traders back to them with the guns and powder to defend themselves against the Pahkees.

In foot racing we were surprised to find there was one young man who was able to match the running of Drouillard and Reubin Fields, who had always easily outdistanced every Indian who tried them. We also played their Indian games, such as prison bases, where each side would try to capture the men who ventured from their base area.

Each day we would ask if the passes were yet open and receive the same answer: We must wait longer. Finally, on June 3, word came that an Indian youth had managed to cross the mountains. Certain that we could go where any Indian could, we decided to leave within a few days. We asked for Indians to guide us, but when none seemed ready to accompany us we determined to set out on our own. Surely Drouillard could guide us through. On June 8 we had a farewell party in our camp on the banks of the Clearwater River. Cruzatte played his fiddle and our Nez Percé friends danced with us late into the night. They were sad to see us go and we were frequently embraced by those good men and women who had grown so close to our own hearts.

That same night, though, we were warned by one of the Nez Percé that we were leaving too soon. He had looked at the trails. Once we were well up into the mountains we would go at least three days without grass for our horses. The way was still too dangerous for us to cross, he said, and we must wait until July. Only then would it be possible.

But our minds were made up. Our leaving could not be postponed again. On June 10, with no Nez Percé to guide us, we rode up the Lolo Trail into the savage Bitterroot Mountains.

It was a mistake.

31

SACAJAWEA

Deep Snow

This is a story the Nez Percé tell. One day, they say, strange creatures came to their villages. Everyone wanted to run away from them. They could make the sound of thunder with their medicine sticks. One of them looked like he had been burned black in a fire. Others of them had eyes like cooked fish and their skins were as pale as snow.

Ah, I do not have to tell any more of that story. You know that they were talking of York and the captains. But it is a good story, my son. It shows that everyone sees the world in a different way.

YOUR UNCLES ALWAYS were so certain that they would succeed, Firstborn Son. Even when they seemed to make mistakes, their spirit helpers always showed them the way to go. But there were times when I almost doubted their judgment. That day when we set out onto the Lolo Trail was one of those times. I knew how much snow could be in the mountains, and without the help of a native guide, we would easily become lost. The Nez Percé had said that they would guide us, but that we still had to wait. Captain Lewis was impatient.

"Let them catch up to us," he said, and then we were off.

Our first day went well, even though it rained hard on us. There was no sign of snow and there were many birds for Captain Lewis to watch and make marks about on his talking leaves. The second day went well, too, at first. We came into a meadow where there was good grass for our horses to eat. That meadow was filled with flowers of all kinds and colors. Captain Lewis got down from his horse to pick flowers, to draw their shapes, and to make many marks about them. Captain Clark explained to me, as he had before when Captain Lewis gathered leaves and flowers and pulled plants up by the roots to take them with him, that some of these flowers were new. No one had ever seen them before, he said. No one had ever named them before.

But they were all flowers I had seen often when I was a small child. I knew their names.

Although the day started well, it did not continue that way. As we climbed higher, we went around a ridge and found nothing but snow ahead of us. Soon the snows grew so deep that they would bury anyone who fell through the crust. For a while we could see where the trail led because the Nez Percé had peeled the bark from the pine trees. That inner bark is good to eat, Firstborn Son, and can help you survive when you are far from other food. But then the snow became so deep that even the trunks of the trees were buried. The trail vanished like a mouse digging into the snow to escape a hawk. In every direction, everything looked the same. Drouillard, who always could find his way before, admitted that he was confused. Captain Lewis, though, did not want to stop. He pushed on.

Each of us, myself included, rode one horse and held the reins of another. As always, your father was the first to get into trouble. His horse stumbled in the snow and threw him into a deep drift, where he sank out of sight. Had he gone over the edge of the trail, he would have rolled off the mountain. All the time that Captain Lewis was digging him out, Charbonneau was calling for help from the *bon Dieu*. But the only help we really needed was to turn around and leave that lost trail.

It did not take your good uncle long to reach that same decision. He spoke to Captain Lewis. We could not go on without a guide. We needed to return while our horses were still strong enough. Captain Lewis was not happy, but he agreed. We made a cache by the trailside and marked it well. In it the captains placed much of their baggage, to pick it up when we came back. Then our party turned and went down the mountain.

◈◇◈

We made camp below the line of snow, where there was good grass for the horses. Then Drouillard and Shannon were sent to get guides from the Nez Percé.

"Tell them," Captain Lewis said, "we will give a good rifle to any man who guides us to the other side of the mountains."

Once again, though, the spirit helpers were smiling on our two captains. Even before Drouillard and Shannon returned to our camp two days later, who should come along but two young Nez Percé boys. Though neither of them had more than sixteen winters, they were on their way to visit friends on the other side of the mountain.

We know this trail well—one of the boys signed—*we can guide you.*

When Drouillard and Shannon returned, they brought

three more young Nez Percé men with them to show us the way.

"We will bring good weather for our journey," the oldest of the young men said. Then he and the other Nez Percé boys set fire to four tall, dry fir trees. The flames and sparks rose high and the smoke carried their prayer for a safe journey up into the sky.

❖❖❖

By the time we reached the place where we had made our cache, we found that the snow was only half as high as it had been when we were there before. Our guides led us across the snows to grassy pastures for our horses and good camping spots. They took us to where Wolf had made a special place when he was shaping the world as the Creator told him to do. The pools of water that come out of the mountain and flow into the river there are always hot, even in the winter. We all warmed ourselves and bathed and played in that water. Our guides truly knew the way well. With them leading us, we crossed the mountains on the Lolo Trail in only half as many days as it had taken us when Old Toby led us toward the sunset.

We made camp in the same place where we had camped during the Moon when Leaves Change Colors. Then the two captains made plans for the last part of our journey. Soon we would be on the rivers that would carry us home. It would be easy for all of us to go together. From this place I knew the trail. I could show them a short way to get to the Great Muddy River.

But once again Captain Lewis had another idea. We had not met the Blackfeet Indians. This, I thought, was a very good thing. The Blackfeet are a dangerous people. They have been given guns by the British. They are afraid of no one and raid our villages and those of the Nez Percé. That is why we call them our worst enemies. I believe it was because their spirit powers were helping them that the two captains had not yet met any Blackfeet—even though we saw many empty Blackfeet camps, the tracks of their horses, and even their distant fires when we traveled toward the sunset.

It was decided that our party would divide into five smaller parties. That way more of the land could be seen. Some of the men would go down the river, to the place where we had left our boats. At the Three Forks, your father and I would separate along with Captain Clark and York and five other men. I would guide them through the mountains along a pass that I knew, until we reached the Yellowstone River. There we would make new canoes and go down the Yellowstone River to the Missouri, coming out close to the Mandan villages.

Our way would not be a hard one to travel. It did not worry me. But the way Captain Lewis planned to travel worried me very much. His plan was to go far to the north of the Great Falls with only nine men. His hope was that he would meet the Blackfeet. He asked our Nez Percé guides to accompany him so that he could make peace between their nations.

"We will not go there," they told him. "The Pahkees do not want peace. If you go, they will cut you off."

In my heart I agreed with them. If Captain Lewis did meet the Blackfeet, I thought, someone would die.

32

WILLIAM CLARK

Five Fingers Parted

Thursday 12th. August 1806

Capt Lewis hove in Sight with the party which went by way of the Missouri as well as that which accompanied him from Travellers rest on Clarks river; I was alarmed on the land of the Canoes to be informed that Capt. Lewis was wounded....

JOURNAL OF WILLIAM CLARK
LITTLE MISSOURI RIVER, NORTH DAKOTA

YOUR MOTHER TOLD YOU HOW we divided into parties on our way back, Pomp? And you wonder why we did so? And you want to know what happened to Captain Lewis with the Blackfeet? Your mother has a way of cracking the shell when she tells a story and then leaving it to me to pry out the meat of the nut.

Yes, the plan was a risky one. We would split off like five fingers parted on a single hand. We would be divided in strength. But every inch of our way was a risk. We were traveling where white men had never dared to go before—though we were followed soon enough by others. In fact, on the last leg of our journey, after our parties had reunited, we met two white men coming upriver. Dickson and Hancock, they were, out of Boone's settlement, heading up the Missouri to trap beaver on the Yellowstone.

Captain Lewis and I talked it over once we were out of the Bitterroots.

"Billy," he said, "it troubles me still about the Blackfeet and the Sioux."

His concern was that those two were the most warlike of all the nations. Everyone else feared them. If our plans for peace among the tribes were to work, making the territory safe for trappers and traders, then something would have to be done about the Blackfeet and the Sioux. Meri and I both had a good opinion of Hugh Heney, the British agent with the Northwest Company, who had a good relation with the Sioux. Of all the white men in the West, Heney seemed liked and trusted the best by the Sioux. When we met him he'd showed some interest in throwing his lot in with the United States. So Meri wrote up a strong letter, asking him to work for us and convince the Sioux to accept peace. Sergeant Pryor and two men set off with that letter and most of our horses. They would go overland to the Mandan villages, give the Indians those horses as a gift, and then deliver the letter to Heney. Traveling free of baggage and with plenty of horses, they'd get there far ahead of everyone else. With luck, by the time we reached the lands of the Sioux, Heney would have spoken with them and brought them into the peace agreement.

That left the Blackfeet to worry about. Captain Lewis proposed to seek them out, taking a party of nine men and seventeen horses along the Great Falls. He would leave three men there to retrieve the things cached at the end of summer and explore the Marias River to the north with the other six.

As for me, one of my concerns was finding a faster and better way from the Missouri to the West. I wanted to avoid that long portage at Great Falls. Your mother had assured me that it was easier to take the Yellowstone River. I would take my part of men as far as the head of the Jefferson River. There we'd stored our canoes before crossing the Lemhi Pass with the Shoshones. There I would strike out toward the Yellowstone with ten men, guided by your good mother. Sergeant Ordway and the other men would take the canoes down Jefferson's River to meet up with Captain Lewis and the others on the Missouri at Great Falls. Then, at the junction of the Yellowstone and the Missouri, the tips of our five fingers would finally meet. If our luck held, we would have in our grasp all that we hoped to accomplish—peace with the hostile tribes and the best knowledge of the ways our nation could travel through the Louisiana Territory.

On July 3 I shook my worthy friend and companion's hand.

"I pray that our separation will be but momentary, Billy," said Captain Lewis. His brave voice was firm and his gaze hopeful, but we clasped each other's hands a bit longer than usual before we each turned to our separate journeys.

❖

My own part of the plan went as smoothly as could be. It was as if I carried the good luck of our Corps of Discovery with me, having you and Janey, your mother, along. As always, York was there by my side, a ready hand whenever he was needed. Your mother knew the way, just as she'd said she did. Without a single misstep, we made our way across a pass through the mountains. We found the Yellowstone, fashioned canoes, and floated down her waters to the Missouri without much trouble at all.

We had gone near a thousand miles since I had last shaken

Captain Lewis's hand. More than a month had passed, and it was now August. But there was no sign of Captain Lewis on the Missouri. We waited for some days, but game was scarce and mosquitoes plentiful. I left a note in a forked stick, as we had done before, and headed downriver to find better hunting.

Finally, at one o'clock on the afternoon of August 12, the canoe and the white pirogue heaved into view. My heart sank, though, when the first word given me by Drouillard was that Meri had been badly wounded.

"The Blackfeet?" I asked.

"No, a hunting accident. Nearsighted Cruzatte mistook his leathers for an elk. He is shot through the hip."

I found my dear friend lying facedown in the white pirogue. He was in great pain and could barely move. But he had kept the presence of mind to dress his wounds in the way best designed to speed their healing.

"Billy," he said, his voice as weak as a child's as he reached a hand to me. "It is so good to see you."

I must admit there were tears in my eyes at seeing my strong friend reduced to such a state. But wounded though his body might be, and disappointed though he might be in his hopes, his spirit was still unconquerable.

"Our friend Cruzatte always has been a finer fiddler than a hunter," he said. "I should thank Providence for that, or he would have hit me in the heart and not the rump." Then he laughed, though I could see that even laughter pained him.

❬❖❭

Gradually, from Captain Lewis and the rest of his party, I learned how two parts of our great plan had failed. To begin with, Sergeant Pryor was there with them in the boats. He and the two men carrying the message to Heney had not gotten far before they lost all their horses to a raiding party of Indians. Making boats from the skins of buffalo, they had floated down the river to join Captain Lewis's men. So no offer of peace had been made to the Sioux. We could expect nothing in the way of friendship from them.

Captain Lewis and his nine men had also lost horses to Indian thieves. Of the seventeen mounts they began with, only seven remained by the time their party reached the Great Falls. There were not enough horses for Meri to take six men with him up the Marias, for spare horses were needed in order to be safe on such a mission. So he chose only three to go with him. They were Drouillard and the two Fields brothers, Joseph and Reubin. With the exception of John Colter, they were the finest of all the woodsmen in our Corps, and the best shots.

The deeper they went into Blackfeet lands, the more worried they became. So small a party and so few weapons would not discourage truly hostile Indians. When at last they did meet a group of eight or nine Indian men and youths, Meri thought them to be Minnetarees at first. In fact, they were Blackfeet. They were hesitant to approach and showed no warmth. Drouillard made the signs of friendship. Then Meri handed out a flag and some medals. It was finally agreed that they would camp together for the night. The Blackfeet built a domed lodge of willow branches and covered it with buffalo skins, inviting our men to join them in the shelter.

Leaving Reubin Fields on watch, Captain Lewis fell into a profound sleep, to be wakened at dawn by the sound of a man shouting.

"Damn you! Let go of my gun!"

It was Drouillard, struggling with one of the Blackfeet who had tried to steal his rifle as he slept. Meri reached for his own rifle. It was gone. Leaping up with his pistol in hand, he saw another of the Indians attempting to get away with his rifle.

Captain Lewis could have shot the man, but he did not. Instead he signaled for him to lay the gun down and back away. The Indian did as he said just as the two Fields brothers came running up, their own rifles at the ready.

By now Drouillard had won back his own gun.

"Let us shoot them, Captain," Drouillard said. He and the Fields brothers were both ready to kill whatever Indians they saw.

"No," Captain Lewis said. "We have our rifles. The Indians are falling back."

He still hoped even then, to avoid a fight. But then he saw the blood on Reubin Fields's shirt.

"What has happened?" Captain Lewis said.

A flood of words came forth from the two brothers. While Reubin slept and Joseph kept watch with his gun lying by his side, two Indians had crept up behind them, grabbing both their guns and running. But the Indians had not accounted for the swiftness of the two brothers, who chased after them and overtook them within sixty paces of the camp. In the struggle to get their guns back, Reubin had pulled his knife and thrust it into the heart of one of the Indians.

"He drew but one breath," Reubin said, "and the wind of his breath followed the knife, and he fell dead."

"The horses!" Captain Lewis said. And it was well he remembered, for the Indians were at that moment trying to steal their horses, leaving them unmounted in that hostile land.

"Shoot the Indians if they try to steal our horses!" Captain Lewis shouted. Then he ran after the men who were driving off the main bunch of the horses. One of the Indians took shelter behind a rock, but the other turned toward Meri and raised his gun, an old British flintlock. Captain Lewis fired, hitting the man in his belly. Though it was a mortal blow, the young Blackfeet warrior still aimed his gun and fired. The ball passed so close to Merry's bare head that he felt the wind of the bullet.

There could be no further peace talks with the Blackfeet. Choosing three of their original horses and four of those left behind by the Blackfeet, Captain Lewis and Drouillard and the Fields brothers galloped south without pausing. But there was no pursuit. They reached the Missouri safely, to rejoin their party.

Did the Blackfeet ever do anything to get even, Pomp? I cannot truly say. Was it that fight that sowed the seeds other men would reap when they came into the lands of the fearsome Blackfeet? It may be so. All I do know is that but a year after our return to St. Louis, Joseph Fields vanished in the Rockies. He was killed, most said, by the Blackfeet. Our dear friend Drouillard returned to the Three Forks of the Missouri to help set up a fur post. And it was near there, a year past, that he lost his life, dying at the hands of the Blackfeet. There was no peace with that nation, and there still is none.

◆◇◆

Just before we headed down the river again on that day of our reuniting, Meri admitted he was too weak to continue his journal.

"Billy," he said, "writing in my present situation is too painful. I must desist. I shall leave the continuation of our journey to you." Then he stared over my shoulder.

"What is it, Meri?" I said, fearing the wound had made him feverish and that he might be seeing things not there.

"Could you bring me," he said, "a branch from that un-usual pin cherry just behind your shoulder?"

Then, as I held it before his face, despite his pain, he man-aged to write a good description of one last botanical specimen before we preserved it to take back with us.

33

SACAJAWEA

This Journey's End

Long ago, they say, the flowers of the prairie were not happy. Back then, whenever flowers died they lost their petals and fell to the earth and their beauty would be gone forever. When people died they walked the Sky Road up into the stars. The flowers felt that this was not fair and they said so to the Great Mystery. The Great Mystery agreed. When it came time for the flowers to die, the Great Mystery made a wind come. It blew those flowers' petals up into the sky. They became the colors of the rainbow.

So it is to this day. The rainbow reminds us that all beautiful things never really die.

IT WAS HAPPY and sad when our parties came back to-gether on the Great Muddy River that day. There was sun in our hearts to see friends we might never have seen again. But the bad wound Captain Lewis had suffered put a cloud over that sunshine. He was trying hard to recover, yet much of the time he was no stronger than you, Firstborn Son. He tried to stand and walk the next day, but his eyes rolled back into his head and he fell to the earth. Your good uncle had to watch out for him as if he were a baby, protecting him and keeping him from doing things that would hurt himself. York and I also spent much of our time by the side of Captain Lewis, helping to care for him. Whenever we pulled ashore, York and Captain Clark would have to lift him from the pirogue, and even though they were slow and gentle as they did this, he was in much pain. He continued to be weak for many days, even after their party left the Mandan villages.

It was sad, too, because our journey was almost over. You and your father and I might soon be parting from the captains. Unless some of the Minnetaree chiefs agreed to accompany the captains on down the river, there would be no need for us as interpreters. This upset your father, Charbonneau, very much. He could no longer imagine what life would be like unless we were in the company of these men who were so filled with curiosity and strength. They had shown courage and great patience on our journey. Even when your father did something foolish, which was often, they would always forgive him. But I did notice that as we came down the river they kept him at the other end of the white pirogue, far away from the rudder.

❖

After the reunion on the river, only two sunrises passed before the big village of the Minnetarees came into view on the right bank of the river. Many people had come to the riverbank to see our arrival. The captains fired the big guns several times. Everyone was glad to see us. People had feared that we were all dead. Rumors had come down the river that we had frozen in the mountains, or that we had been wiped out by the Pahkees or taken prisoner by other white men who hated the Americans.

Black Moccasin, the chief of Meteharta, the Village of the Willows, where your father and I had been living before we met the captains, stood on the bank. He began weeping as our boats came to shore. But his tears were not those of gladness.

"I weep because my son is dead," Black Moccasin said. "He was killed by the Blackfeet."

Your father was sent to ask the various Minnetaree chiefs to gather for a meeting. Drouillard was sent downstream to the Mandan villages to bring back their chiefs and Jessaume the interpreter. Soon everyone was in the big council lodge. Even Captain Lewis was there, though he was not strong enough to speak. Your good uncle Captain Clark hoped to convince the chiefs to come with him to Washington. But things were not good. The ideas of peace put forward by the captains had not succeeded.

Black Moccasin spoke and told how things were. Soon after the captains had left, the Sioux had raided the Minnetarees and killed eight of them. The Arikaras had raided to steal many horses, and the Minnetarees had killed two Arikaras in turn. The Blackfeet continued to raid them from the north. It seemed as if everyone was at war.

"If the Sioux were at peace," Black Moccasin said, "and could be depended on, I would be glad to go and see the Great Father. But we are afraid of the Sioux and thus we will not go."

Though Captain Clark tried hard to convince them, none of the Minnetarees or the Mandans wanted to go down the river with them. It was clear that our jobs as interpeters were ended.

"Sacre," Charbonneau said, "to say *adieu,* my heart it will break."

Though I did not speak, I felt, too, as if a part of my heart was being taken from me. The white men had treated me with friendship and respect always, and I could not imagine ever meeting so fine a company of men again. You had become like a grandchild to Captain Clark. He had watched you grow now for two years. His eyes were always on you in those last days we were together. He would drop to one knee and hold out his hands. Then you would run to him on your strong little legs, as if you were dancing. You would grasp his leather jacket, begging him to lift you and throw you up into the air.

When I closed my eyes, I could no longer see the face of my own father clearly. So many winters had passed since that day at the Three Forks when the Minnetarees stole me from my family. But your good uncle had given me back what was left of my family. He had brought me back to my brother and the land of my birth and our people. I realized that I would always be able to remember the smiling face of Captain Clark. He had become a second father.

◆◇◆

Only two days passed before it was time for them to leave. Captain Clark paid your father well for his services. He even offered to take us with them down to the Illinois if we wished. But your father turned down Captain Clark's kind offer.

"I would have no acquaintance there," Charbonneau said. "I would have no way to make a living. I must continue to live in the way I have done."

"Janey," Captain Clark said to me, "you deserve a greater reward for your attention and services than we have in our power to give you."

I said nothing in return. Our people have no words to say good-bye.

Then your good uncle held you in his arms one last time. "Pomp," he said, "my beautiful, promising, dancing boy."

Your hands on each side of his big face, your little fingers in his red hair, you looked up into his eyes. And Captain Clark's eyes were moist as he looked back at you.

"My dear friends," he said to us, "I want to ask you for a great favor. I want to take your son. Not now, but perhaps in a year, when he is weaned? I would raise him in such a manner as I think proper. He would want for nothing. Can you bring Pomp to me?"

Neither Charbonneau nor I hesitated. Though we both love you very much, we knew what a good life Captain Clark would give you. It was because we loved you that we wanted this for you. We agreed to bring you to him in the future. And then we parted.

34

WILLIAM CLARK

∞∞∞∞∞∞∞∞∞∞∞∞∞∞∞∞∞∞∞∞∞∞

Old Friends No Longer with Us

Saturday 20th Septr. 1806

Every person, both French and americans seem to express great pleasure at our return, and acknowledged themselves much astonished in seeing us return. they informed us that we were supposed to have been lost long since, and were entirely given out by every person &c.

JOURNAL OF WILLIAM CLARK
ST. LOUIS

YES, POMP, OUR JOURNEY CONTINUED after your good mother's ended at the Mandan village. There we left you and your parents, with no little regret, though in hopes of a future reunion. Of our men, only John Colter stayed behind. We granted him an early discharge so that he might go back up the river with the two trappers we had met on our way down. Since then, Colter's own adventures—and wonderful stories— have added much to the map of the West that we drew.

As we continued down the river, Captain Lewis continued to improve in health.

Our one great fear was that the Sioux would attempt to

stop our passage. So we swept past their main village on the river as fast as we could, keeping our boats well to the opposite bank and our weapons ready. Though they waved their arms at us and begged us to stop, we did not pause.

"You are bad people," Jessaume shouted at them.

At that, one of their great chiefs climbed to a hill and struck his war bow against the ground as he stared at us. This, we were told, was a great oath and showed his anger.

❖

On we went, stopping briefly with the Arikaras but never slowing our progress more than a day or so. At last, on a day I shall never forget—September 20 it was—we knew that we were almost home. There, on the banks of the river, we saw cows grazing.

We were welcomed with joy and astonishment. All thought we had been lost. Some had said we were killed by the Indians. Others had heard that the Spanish had taken us prisoner and that we were captives, doomed to slave the rest of our lives in their mines. I would later discover, Pomp, that such might have been the case had we gone farther south. The Spanish knew of our journey and had sent parties of men out to capture us, though none ever came close.

Much had happened while we were gone. We were as hungry for even the smallest bit of news as a starving man is for a crust of bread. The strangest thing was to hear that Aaron Burr, the vice president of the United States, had killed the secretary of the treasury, Alexander Hamilton, in a duel. The best news was that our great president, Thomas Jefferson, had been elected again to office. You see, Pomp, among our people a man is not chief forever. He serves for a time at the wish of the people and then retires to be just like other men.

Yes, it must be hard for someone who has been a chief to return to being just like other men again.

We were feted and toasted by the whole town of St. Louis at a great dinner and ball held at Christy's Inn. Everyone made us welcome, and it seemed as if every home in this fair city was open to us. Then, in November, we were on our way again. President Jefferson had written Meri telling him of the "unspeakable joy" he felt at the news of his safe return. Captain Lewis was to hurry to Monticello and then to Washington. When he arrived there, our president welcomed Captain Lewis, who was like a son to him, with the greatest warmth. Meri had with him our journals and our maps. They spent long hours talking of the great discoveries and got down together on their hands and knees in the president's house to pore over the great map we had made of the West. In Washington Meri was treated as a great hero, which indeed he was.

As for myself, I went not to Washington but to Virginia. My mind had often been on my friends in Fincastle, and on one young Julia Hancock in particular. Yes, Pomp, you know her. She consented to be my wife.

During that time I was away from Meri, I fear that things began to go awry. With so much celebration and not enough work to fill the day, Meri took to drinking too heavily. After each bout of drinking he felt great shame and vowed to stop, but he always broke his vow.

Then Jefferson gave him the honor of the governorship of Louisiana, and Meri returned to St. Louis in 1808. I had been placed in charge of Indian affairs for the territory. I planned to arrive from Virginia some time after Meri, who had been expected in Louisiana a full year before he finally got there. He had lingered longer than expected, first in Washington and then in Philadelphia and then in Virginia. He had courted first one young woman and then another. He longed to be married as I was, but each romance ended in failure. We all, even President Jefferson, were greatly concerned about him.

◄◆►

The house Meri chose for us in St. Louis was a grand home on Spruce and South Main. There was plenty of room for Julia and myself to move in with him. Our year together in that house brought me great blessings. Not only was I with my dear friend, but Julia gave birth to our first son. Yes, I am speaking of little Meri. Meriwether Lewis Clark.

But though my own life filled with great joy, Pomp, things did not work out for Meri as he had planned. Jealous men who worked for him told lies about him. His drinking became worse and his debts grew. He began taking heavy doses of medicine so that he could sleep at night. Though he had promised to publish our journals, he kept putting off the editing of them. He fell into despair. It became necessary to make a trip to Washington to try to solve his problems and put his accounts in order. He hoped, also, to finally finish the editing of our journals, and took them with him.

I, too, was going to Washington, for I had business with the War Department. I suggested that we travel together, but Meri felt that we should take different routes, just as we did from Travelers' Rest.

"We shall come at them from land and from sea, Billy," he said. He feared that the British planned to steal his journals and thought two trails would be harder to follow than one.

We parted, and I would never see him again. As he traveled along the Natchez Trace he fell again into drinking and despair. Stopped for the night at a small inn in Tennessee, he shot himself with his pistol, then slashed his body with his razor. It took him all night to die.

His journals and the word of his tragic end were brought to me. I was told that he had cried out for me, saying that I would soon arrive and save him. I wept, and I shall weep again at the thought of his bright light vanishing from this world. Though I have not the ability to edit our journals, it shall be done. I shall see them published, and the world will know how great were the accomplishments of my truest friend.

Others of our old friends from that great Corps of Discovery are no longer with us. I have kept a list of the expedition members and shall do so until I take my own final journey, Pomp. Here are the names of all those of whom I still know. Sergeant Floyd, the only one of our fortunate company to perish on our journey. George Drouillard, killed by the Blackfeet. Private Labiche, who went with Meri to Washington, now back here in St. Louis. John Colter, gone now to Missouri to marry. Sergeant Gass has stayed on in the army, as has Private McNeal. Two good men to fight the British, should it come to that again. John Shields, our blacksmith and gunsmith, trapping in Missouri with his kinsman Daniel Boone. Sergeant Pryor, busy in the Indian trade on the Missouri. Private Weiser, killed by the Blackfeet. George Shannon, now at the university, studying to be a lawyer. Joseph Fields, killed in the Rockies, and his brother Reubin gone back to Kentucky. I could go on. But here in my home are now gathered four of our brave party, since you and your parents are with me.

What is that you say, Pomp? No, you are right and I am wrong. There are five of us here. York is one. York always was one of us. You know, Pomp, the things that you and your mother have said to me of late about my companion have stuck to me like a burr in a sock. It has always seemed to me that perpetual involuntary servitude is contrary to the principles of natural justice. And I know how much York has ached to be his own man, ill prepared for it though he may still be.

Have you not noticed how happy our old friend seemed this morning? It is because I just told him that I have prepared these papers. You see these here, Pomp? Manumission papers. That means I am granting him his freedom. He means to go to Tennessee, where his wife—herself a slave—and their children live. I've allowed him to save enough money to purchase their freedom and some small place to live. I am also giving him a large wagon and a team of six horses so that he can employ himself. I am glad that it makes you happy, my boy. I just hope it proves to be happy for York.

35

SACAJAWEA

〰〰〰〰〰〰〰〰〰

The Final Word

We must always be careful of the water. When we travel on it, we must always be sure to respect it and give it thanks for a safe journey. Not only is the water alive, there are powerful beings who live within the waters. Those are the ones we call the Water Babies. If you do not show respect, then they will tip over your canoe and you will drown. If you show respect, they will not bother you. You will travel safely. You will survive your journey and return again to those who love you.

YES, MANY THINGS HAPPENED to Captain Clark in the days that fell between then and now. Much that was good and bad came into his life, things that made his heart fill with sun and other things that brought the clouds around his head. With one thing and another, more than a year had passed. But we brought you at last to the house of your good uncle, here in St. Louis. And here you have heard the great story of our journey, a journey like no other. It is a story for you to hold in your heart, my son, a story to keep your heart good and make your spirit strong. But now we have come to this journey's end.

We have had a good stay in this place. Captain Clark's wife has been kind to us. She has always placed plenty of food on her table. She has made it clear that there is plenty of room in her home for you. But your father and I both know the life in a city or on a white man's farm is not the life he and I were meant to lead. Charbonneau wishes to travel again.

And, it seems, so do I. The river is still speaking to me, ready to carry me away. Like all of those who made that great journey, your mother, too, was changed. I had dreamed of traveling when I was young. I had asked the river to carry me with it. But when my travels began, they were far harder than I could ever have imagined. It is also true that although much was lost to me when I was forced to leave my people behind, the path I followed had much to teach me. That path led through rapids that sought to swallow me and grind my bones on the teeth of their sharp stones. It led over mountains so cold that my blood was ready to freeze, and to the endless salt water that held more power than I had ever experienced before. But that path also led into the heart. I learned to see with clear eyes into my own heart and into the hearts of others. I learned courage. So your mother is still eager to see different places, to hear words spoken in other languages, to sit around the fire in distant camps. Our Numi women have always been strong, my son. But one never knows how much strength one truly has until that strength is tested. I found that my strength was enough to carry me there and back safely—and to carry you as well.

Perhaps this time I will go no farther than the Mandan towns. Or maybe I will return again to the Three Forks and see if my brother is still waiting for my return. Whatever our destination, it is certain that soon your father and I will go back up the river. Now, if you wish to remain here, you can stay. But remember, Firstborn Son, my stories, especially the great story of the journey we shared, will always be with you. Like a mother's love, they will travel with you wherever you choose to go.

Author's Note

ONE OF THE QUESTIONS ASKED of writers of historical novels is this: How much of your story is history and how much is fiction? The answer depends not only on the research done (or not done) by the writer, but also on what sources are available. In some cases, nothing was written down at the time when the events took place—or, even worse, the story was only chronicled years later by someone with no firsthand knowledge.

There is no shortage of firsthand testimony about the Lewis and Clark Expedition. Of all the expeditions made in the nineteenth century, none was better recorded at the exact time it happened than the epic journey of the Corps of Discovery, as they called themselves. President Thomas Jefferson, the driving force behind the journey, described it somewhat disingenuously to the Spanish ambassador as being "purely literary" in its scope. Indeed, every literate person who took part was urged to keep a diary, and a good many of them did. Apparently some of those written accounts were lost. But more survived. First of all, there are the extensive journals of the two captains themselves, thousands of pages of minutely detailed observation, with Lewis beginning his on August 30, 1803, and Clark ending his on "Moday June 9th 1806" [sic]. We also have in print the three-volume journal of Sergeant John

Ordway, the journal of Sergeant Patrick Gass, and the less-extensive diaries of Sergeant Charles Floyd and Private Joseph Whitehorse. Anyone attempting to write about any aspect of the Lewis and Clark Expedition would be foolhardy not to read the magnificent eight-volume set of the journals, diaries, field notes, and maps edited by Gary E. Moulton and published as *The Journals of the Lewis & Clark Expedition* by the University of Nebraska. I also strongly recommend James P. Ronda's highly insightful *Lewis and Clark Among the Indians*, also from the University of Nebraska Press.

I have attempted to be absolutely true to the journals whenever I refer to events taking place on the journey, whether my narrator is William Clark or Sacajawea. This holds true even for the dialogue, which is drawn directly from the journals. Here, for example, is part of a Meriwether Lewis journal entry from Monday, August 12, 1805, followed by my adaptation of it in this novel:

JOURNAL:
Two miles below McNeal had exultingly stood with a foot on each side of this little rivulet and thanked his god that he had lived to bestride the mighty & heretofore deemed endless Missouri....

NOVEL:
McNeal stood laughing with one foot on either side of that stream which had seemed so endless.

"Dear Lord, I do thank you," McNeal said, "for allowing me to live long enough to bestride the mighty Missouri."

Insofar as the names of the many Native American nations encountered by the Corps of Discovery are concerned, I have also—whenever Clark is speaking—used the names given them by Lewis and Clark, even though these are not the names those nations call themselves. Thus the Hidatsa are called Minnetaree, the Piegan are called Blackfeet, the Lakota are called Sioux, the Nu-Mee-Poom are Nez Percé, and so on. In the case of the many nations along the Columbia River, there is so much uncertainty (both at the time of the expedition and among present-day researchers) as to which of the many peoples were actually encountered on any given date, that I have referred to them as "River Indians." Both Lewis and Clark were constantly changing the spelling and even the names of the various nations they met. Thus Sacajawea's Numi were first referred to as "Snakes," then "Cho-sho-ne," then "Sosone," and finally "Shoshone." To make it less confusing, I have chosen one name in every case and stuck with it. In Sacajawea's half of the narrative, these people are sometimes referred to differently, reflecting her differing viewpoint. Pahkees, for example, is the name Sacajawea's people gave to the Blackfeet and the other nations that raided her people (probably derived from *pakihi'i*, meaning "stiff, hardened blanket," a reference to the rawhide shields and armor used by the Blackfeet in battle).

And what about those who kept no journal, Sacajawea in particular? Again, I have always referred closely to events chronicled during and after the expedition. If you look into the journals you will find every happening in this novel that involves Sacajawea, even though her understanding of it may not be the same as Clark's. I have tried to make sure that the events as she describes them are seen through a Native eye. The stories she tells are all traditional tales, either from her own people or other nations encountered along the way. Moreover, the framing device of the novel squares with history. Clark did, indeed, invite Sacajawea, Charbonneau, and Pomp to his home in St. Louis, and they did eventually come. I have imagined the scenario of Pomp asking them to tell him the story of the journey, as a very bright and well-loved child might do. However, it is true that Pomp, Jean Baptiste Charbonneau, remained in the white world long enough to be educated, travel to Europe, and return to the West, where he became a famous and respected guide. His name turns up again and again in chronicles of the period.

There is also historical documentation in the volume *In Search of York* by Robert B. Betts (Colorado Associated UP, 1985) about Clark's questionable treatment of his companion and faithful servant following the expedition, and York's eventual manumission from slavery.

I have turned to the history, stories, and traditions of the Shoshone for more information about the character of Sacajawea, to gain insight into what she might have thought or said about her experience. I'm grateful to Wayland Large, the Tribal Historian of the Wind River Shoshones, for his helpful comments on her story, her "Hidatsa" name, and the Shoshone language. Though most white historians believe Sacajawea died shortly after her visit to St. Louis, Shoshone oral tradition says with great certainty that she lived a long life, traveled far, and is buried there at Wind River. Charles Eastman, the Nakota Sioux writer, went around the West during the early 1900s to collect the numerous stories about Sacajawea's survival and the events of her later life when she became known as "Woman Chief." One of her contemporary relatives, Eileen Charbonneau, concurs with that version of Sacajawea's story. Eileen was kind enough to read this manuscript and offer her comments as well.

It has been my good fortune over the years to have been

taught by a number of Native American elders, women who have been storytellers and tradition keepers. I think that any strength to be found in Sacajawea's voice, as I have imagined it, comes in part from them. But it also comes from the history. Imagine yourself to be Sacajawea, a teenage mother in the company of men traveling rivers and mountains without end, enduring hunger and pain and danger, and not only doing it without complaint but contributing on numerous occasions to the success and well-being of the company. The Sacajawea that we find if we look closely at the things recorded about her by those who traveled with her is an admirable, strong-minded, resilient woman—the best sort of person to have as a mother or as a friend.

Selected Bibliography

Ambrose, Stephen E. *Undaunted Courage: Meriwether Lewis, Thomas Jefferson, and the Opening of the American West.* New York: Simon & Schuster, 1996.

Beckwith, Martha W., ed. *Mandan-Hidatsa Myths and Ceremonies.* Vol. 32, *Memoirs of the American Folklore Society.* New York: G. E. Stechert & Co., 1938.

Betts, Robert B. *In Search of York: The Slave Who Went to the Pacific with Lewis and Clark.* Boulder, Colo.: Colorado Associated Univ. Press, 1985.

Boas, Frank, ed. *Chinook Texts.* Washington, D.C.: Smithsonian Institution, BAE Bulletin no. 20, 1894.

Clark, Ella E., comp. *Indian Legends from the Northern Rockies.* Norman, Okla.: Univ. of Oklahoma Press, 1966.

Clark, Ella E., and Margot Edmonds. *Sacajawea of the Lewis and Clark Expedition.* Berkeley, Calif.: Univ. of California Press, 1980.

Duncan, Dayton, and Ken Burns. *Lewis & Clark: The Journey of the Corps of Discovery.* New York: Knopf, 1997.

Howard, Harold P. *Sacajawea.* Norman, Okla.: Univ. of Oklahoma Press, 1971.

Moulton, Gary E., ed. *The Journals of the Lewis and Clark Expedition.* Lincoln, Nebr.: Univ. of Nebraska Press, 1983–1991.

Robinson, Sheila C., comp. *Along the Lewis & Clark Trail in North Dakota.* BHG Inc., 1993.

Ronda, James P. *Lewis and Clark among the Indians.* Lincoln, Nebr.: Univ. of Nebraska Press, 1984.

Thwaites, Rueben Gold, ed. *Original Journals of the Lewis and Clark Expedition, 1804–1806.* New York: Dodd & Mead Co., 1904–1905.

Trenholm, Virginia Cole, and Maurine Carley. *The Shoshonis: Sentinels of the Rockies.* Norman, Okla.: Univ. of Oklahoma Press, 1964.

Wilson, Gilbert L. (as told to). *Buffalo Bird Woman's Garden: Agriculture of the Hidatsa Indians.* Saint Paul: Minnesota Historical Society Press, 1987.

I also recommend a visit to the web site of the *Bismarck Tribune*, where Tribune Innovations Editor Ken Rogers has written an extremely interesting series of well-researched articles entitled *Sakakawea and the Fur Traders.* One article includes a discussion of the assertion in oral traditions at Fort Berthold that Sakakawea was not Shoshone at all but a Hidatsa woman.

www.ndonline.com/TribWebPage/Sakakawea/sakakindex.html